To my parents, husband and children for their love and support.

Chapter 1

In the beginning was God, and within God was the very thought of you. With patience and great care, he brought you forth and established your future. Indeed, all things, both seen and unseen, have their existence in God. He is the seed of all life, the source of all reality. He is the center of all gravity and upholds the entire whirling universe. He has always been, will always be, and is without beginning or ending. He is everywhere, is ever-expanding, and delights in his entire creation. He is love generously dispersed, kindness radiating eternally, joy infinitely magnified, truth overcoming all error, goodness softening our hearts, and Spirit dwelling within us.

God has been called many names: Heavenly Father, Divine Mother, Allah, Jehovah, Vishnu, Universal Mind, Higher Power, Everlasting Love, and Spirit of Truth, among others. The names we use often depend on our upbringing or how we have grown to understand the Divine. Although God is spirit and transcends all genders, we can relate to our Creator in both masculine and feminine terms. The names and pronouns we use, though, are not what is important. What matters is that we have an open mind and a receptive heart. What matters is that we wish to know more about the goodness and grandeur of our Creator. What matters is that we have a desire to know more about the design of our universe, why we are here, and where we are going. What matters is that we are seekers of truth and are willing to search for answers both within and without. What matters is that we wish to know God, because in knowing him we will come to love him.

One of the most remarkable revelations given to us about the nature of God is that he can be thought of as a loving parent. There is no more tender relationship than between a parent and a child, and it is with this same affection that God cares for us. He gives freely of himself, is selfless toward his children, and is full of goodness and compassion. He is a Heavenly Parent reaching out to experience life with us and through us.

If you were taught growing up to believe you are a child of God, it may be easy to consider a Creator who is like a loving parent. If you have a positive image of your earthly mother or father, it may be natural for you to think of God in loving terms. It may be easy for you to remember all the ways your parents cared for you, provided for you, and made you feel loved, secure, and accepted. You may not have known it at the time, but your parents were reflecting God to you.

Or perhaps you had a strong grandparent who raised you. If so, you may think of God in terms of a loving older relative, but you should resist the image of God with long white hair resting somewhere up in the clouds. For God is no Cosmic Senior Citizen looking down on us from a celestial assisted-living home.

He is the one who designed the entire universe, thought us into existence, is present within us, and loves us for all eternity. He exists beyond age, gender, race, religion, or any label we might use to separate and divide. Indeed, God is the Great Uniter, our universe is One, and we exist within her like a child within a mother's womb.

Like God, good parents are nurturing and love us unconditionally. They patiently watch over us and do not allow us to stubbornly go our own way. They establish boundaries to protect us in a troubled world. They make our welfare a priority. They oversee our upbringing and education. They protect us from indulging in things that might harm us. They care about our well-being. They speak positive words over us and fill us with hope and encouragement. They help us form a positive self-image and pay no mind to our momentary shortcomings. They believe in us and love us through every stage of growth and development.

As much as our earthly parents love us, though, their knowledge of us is partial, and their power to protect us is limited. But with God, there are no limits. His knowledge is complete, and his power is infinite. So while parents may watch over us for a while, God watches over us forever. Parents make plans that will carry their children into adulthood, but God makes plans that will carry us into eternity. At some point we must release our children to God's care and trust that he will guide and protect them. At some point we must release ourselves to God's care as well.

But how do we do this? How do we trust God with our lives and our loved ones? How do we disengage from the distractions and pleasures of the world to make time for the Divine? How do we release our fears long enough to take hold of God's hand? The answer is: gradually. Our acceptance and understanding of God takes time; this is a primary purpose of evolution. God grants us time in abundance, from life to life and from here to eternity. So even though we must continue to work, care for our families, meet our responsibilities, and survive on planet Earth, we must also learn to declutter our days, make room for God, and discover his bountiful love.

When we simplify our lives, we allow for inner experiences that can connect us to God. Our spiritual journeys can begin voluntarily, with a desire to understand the cosmic design for our lives, but they can also begin with a crisis. When we go through difficult times, we are more likely to call out to the one who can alleviate our pain. When we are at a loss to understand why there is so much suffering in the world, we are more likely to ponder the idea of a Creator. In our hour of greatest need, we are more likely to pray and seek answers from a divine source.

Our journey as humans began long, long ago, but now we are awakening to a new phase of the journey. Even though there are untold hardships throughout the world and the potential for catastrophic change due to global war, global warming, and the destruction of our natural resources, we should not accept that the grand experiment of evolution is almost over. We should not assume we know the endgame or presume God is admitting defeat; he is just getting started. Evolution is long, but eternity is longer. So, before we're tempted to give up, let's begin a conversation with our Creator. Let's ask what this is all about. Let's find out who's in charge. Let's wake up each morning expecting to have our prayers answered, our fears erased, and our joy renewed.

Developing a rich inner life begins by carving time out of your day for quiet contemplation, prayer, and meditation. It begins by treating your relationship with God like other important relationships in your life and choosing to spend time with him. The more time you spend with someone, the more you begin to appreciate their presence. If, however, you take them for granted, or put little or no effort into the relationship, you naturally reap few positive rewards. We all reap in proportion to how we sow.

There is a depth and breadth to everyone, and if we draw near, listen, and seek to truly understand another, we can transcend the superficial boundaries that keep us apart. When we have a desire to know someone more deeply, then we drop all pretenses and exchange shallow small talk for more meaningful ways of relating and communicating. In the same way, if we want a deeper connection with God, we must become more genuine and sincere in our efforts.

As much as God desires to be known, he will never compel you to turn to him. He will not force you into a relationship. He will draw you near to help you acknowledge his love for you, but he has made you a freethinker. He has given you a free will, and he respects the long, slow, process of discovery. He trusts that in time you will find peace within and peace with him.

You cannot know all that awaits you by your simple act of choosing—choosing to go within, to reach out to God, to begin a relationship with him, and to consider that the universe is lovingly designed and administered. God reaches out through time and space to be with us, grow with us, and help transform our lives into something more beautiful than we can now imagine. God has no limiting qualities and no existence outside of love. Yet his Spirit lives within us, always counseling, always comforting, always working to awaken us to his presence and improve our lives.

You cannot predict all the good in store for you and all the adventures prepared for you, unless you are first willing to take a step of faith to connect with God. What does a step of faith look like? It looks like trust. It looks like daring to believe in an invisible Creator. It looks like moving forward into the unknown. It looks like making decisions without the help of a crystal ball, an astrology chart, or a psychic to predict your future. It looks like following a small voice within. It looks like responding to a faint idea, a spark of hope, a gentle nudge, or a kind inner counselor. It looks like daring to move forward, stepping out of your comfort zone, or dedicating yourself to a task when there's no guarantee of a reward. It looks like accepting that all things are working together for your highest good, despite life's many sorrows and uncertainties. It looks like walking down a moonlit path and seeing only a few feet ahead of you, rather than standing on a mountaintop and surveying a sweeping, sunlit landscape.

Excluding God from your life and your decision making is like going to a five-star restaurant and asking the waiter, who has no experience working in a kitchen, to prepare your meal. Why would you do that when there's an award-winning chef on staff? Or it's like going to a five-star hotel, paying for your accommodations, and then choosing to pitch a tent outside on the sidewalk. Why would you choose the hard pavement when you can have a comfortable sleep experience inside? But that's what can happen when we choose to make plans without God— we waste money, time, and resources. Or imagine getting a full scholarship to the college of your choice, but turning it down in favor of staying home because you're too scared of change, too doubtful of your own abilities, and too afraid to commit to a plan of action.

God can easily help you overcome your fears and advance in life, if only you will reach out to him. Do you want to lead a better life? Then why ignore the one who can help you the most? When hard choices confront you, when you want to know the direction for your life, when a crisis overtakes you, when you've lost all sense of hope or humor, when you become entangled with difficult personalities, when you struggle with an addiction, or when you are confronted with bad news—stop, breathe, and consider your Creator. He is gentle, kind, and understanding. Trust God to comfort you. Trust that he has an amazing future planned for you, and that future begins now. Take a moment to talk to God.

We are in a realm of existence where the majority of the universe is unseen. Due to the limits of our human eyes and the limits of our technology, we can only see so much. Eventually, more of the cosmos will open up to us, but much will remain unseen. There must be a reason God has placed us here with such limited vision and understanding. He has infinite intelligence and created the entire swirling universe, yet here we are on Earth— feeble, finite, and visually impaired. So naturally, we must ask ourselves, why?

It seems God takes great pleasure in creating and sustaining, in making something out of nothing, in taking the unseen and making it visible to all. He takes a thought, a word, a note, an atom, a cell, a seed, an egg, and builds endlessly upon it. He takes what is vulnerable and raises it to an exalted status. He takes what is weak and foils the critics. He turns a tiny embryo into an adult. He makes an oak tree rise from a seed. He births a solar system from a sun, and has a universe pour forth from his thoughts. He sets humans down on Earth, and then lifts them up to the heavens. Now we are a little lower than the angels, but in time we will rise to new heights, because God delights in making all things new.

Though we may at times feel weak and lowly, God has only just begun a good work in us. He has placed us here for a season, to learn priceless lessons and to establish an eternal foundation. It is here, on this earth, where we are first challenged to believe in an invisible God. It is here where we begin to grow into our unique personalities. It is here, in a world filled with pain and disappointment, where we learn to become courageous and hopeful. It is here where we learn to go against the grain of millions of years of biological struggle to become selfless. It is here where we come to know our own strength. It is here where we learn to trust one another and form community. It is here where we learn the lessons of family, friendship, and faith.

Jesus, who has been called the incarnation of God and one of the greatest spiritual teachers of our world, once taught one of his most valuable lessons by directing attention to a child. "Truly I tell you, unless you change and become like little children, you will never enter the kingdom of heaven. Therefore, whoever humbles himself like this child is the greatest in the kingdom of heaven, and whoever welcomes a child like this, welcomes me."

Did he mean that we are to become naïve, childish, and immature? No, in becoming like little children, we are to begin trusting God like a father, a papa, a parent. We are to begin allowing him to lovingly lead us. We are to have a simplicity of belief and open ourselves up to his provision and affection.

Children naturally trust their parents, and God would have us enter into a similar parent-child relationship with him.

Everyone has equal access to God. This spiritual opportunity is completely independent of your religion, race, nationality, language, gender, sexual orientation, education, social standing, or circumstances. It does not matter how rich or poor, how confident or broken, how weak or strong, how young or old, how this or that; if you have a desire in your heart to reach out to God and connect with him, he will welcome you with open arms. He doesn't ask anything but a sincere heart and a small willingness on your part. Whether you are at home, away at school, in a hospital, in a prison cell, on an airplane, on the road, on an island, on the open sea, or in a bustling city, it matters not. He will come to you.

God can break into your life at any place, any time, any age, regardless of outer affairs. His timing does not depend upon the state of the world, which political party is in power, whether there is war or peace, capitalism or communism, disease or health, extreme weather or calm, good times or bad. All that matters is your honest decision to accept God's unconditional love. Nothing in all of creation can separate you from his love, so decide today to take God's hand. Decide you want to begin life anew.

Faith is all that is required to connect to your Creator. Is there even a grain of belief in you? Then say, like the man who asked Jesus to perform a miracle and heal his son, "I believe; help my unbelief!" God does not ask that we have faith that will move mountains. He asks that we have the faith of a child. He asks that we simply invite him into our lives. Open the door of your heart today, and allow him to gently greet you. If you struggle to believe, it only means you are entirely human, for no one on Earth is infallible. Every person on Earth has experienced doubt and disbelief. Everyone on Earth wrestles with the truth and searches for answers. Ask God to help your unbelief.

When we seek the truth, we will find God, and then we will begin to know the truth of who we are. When we join God's spiritual family, when we enter the kingdom of God, our status will not suddenly change from being lost to found, orphaned to adopted, or condemned to redeemed, because God has never seen us as lost, orphaned, or condemned. God will open our eyes to show us that we have always been his beloved children. From the beginning we have been a part of his family. From the beginning he has had his hand outstretched to us. From the beginning he has been guiding us gently to himself. From the beginning he has held a privileged place for us and planned our remarkable future.

So enter the kingdom of heaven within, and freely receive the keys to God's house. Here you do not have to beg, bargain, or bribe your way in. Your father built and owns the house, and he joyfully shares all that he has with his children. You and your brothers and sisters can enter in with confidence and gladness, knowing it is your home too. Here you can feel welcome and safe and part of an expansive, loving family. And for all eternity you can enjoy the fullness of God's love, the abundance of his provision, and the many rooms of his mansion.

In God's house, he uses time as a blanket and stretches it out over our lives. He covers us as we sleep and then gently awakes us. He fills our days with opportunities to play, explore, learn, and serve. He never tires of being our Heavenly Parent. He lives to share his love and still our minds when we are scared. He guides us in the direction of peace without force or compulsion. He creates the conditions for our material and spiritual progress. He uses time as a means to renew, heal, perfect, and unite all things. His ways may seem slow, but the outcome is sure.

All that we would label past, present, and future are as one to God, for time is his invention. It is one of his great creative constructs, and he has measured out a portion for all. He has allowed us to decide how we will use the time allotted us. Will time fly by or stand still? Will we be ahead of our time or behind the times? Oblivious to time or a slave to time? Just in time or out of time? The choice to turn to God is a choice to save time, to awaken, to no longer waste time, and to enter into the joy he has planned for you. It is a choice to make a quantum leap forward in understanding God's perfect plan for us all.

Welcoming God into your life will set you on a new course of living. With an awareness of God, old ways of thinking will dissolve, fruitless plans will come to an end, and former ambitions will fall away in favor of more excellent ones. The harsh outer edges of your personality will soften. You will remember once again what it is to have a pure heart, a clean conscience, a sure purpose, and the simple faith of a child. You will emerge from the aged cocoon of selfish living to begin a new life of concern for others. You will want to do good, and you will desire to help improve the lives of those around you. With God's love welling up within you, you will naturally love yourself and others more. You will be attuned to God's voice, and you will slowly turn away from all that would distract you from his perfect ways. You will seek his advice on how best to use your time to make the world a better place, and you will be led to shed old habits and worn-out ways of thinking. Gradually, you will develop a more profound sense of God's presence, a love for all living things, and a desire to improve the quality of life for all.

By remaining humble, prayerful, and attentive to where God's Spirit is leading you, you will begin to make wiser choices that will lead to more productive living. You will begin to establish boundaries and better organize your days to fulfill your calling. You will learn how to persist, overcome obstacles, move beyond defeat, and live courageously. You will learn how to tap into an endless fountain of energy, goodness, and wisdom found within you. You will learn how to bring heaven to mind, heaven into your home, and heaven to Earth.

What distracts you from hearing God's call for your life? What turns you away from him? Are you caught up in a busy lifestyle that provides no time for God? Are you working too hard? Are you dreaming too little? Are you out of balance? Do little sins keep you away from a relationship with him? Do larger sins keep you in a place of shame or darkness? No matter where you are in life, no matter what you've done, God is available to you at all times.

Pause, pray, and quiet your mind. Begin today to connect with your Creator. It will be the start of a bold, new adventure. Do not think that because God is spirit, he cannot be known, or that because the universe is so vast, it is not perfectly planned and administered. Do not think that because you are so small, you do not matter. Do not think that because your troubles are so great, there is no divine plan for your life. Your thoughts are heard, your steps are guided, and your future is guaranteed. Begin today to trust God, and allow yourself to believe the fantastic—that the Creator of this whole, wide universe knows you and loves you like a Heavenly Parent. Won't you open your heart and receive this love today?

Chapter 2

For some it may take a great leap of faith to believe in a loving God with whom you can have a personal relationship. For some it may take a leap of faith to believe the universe is perfectly ordered and administered. For some it may take a leap of faith to believe in evolution. For others it may take a leap of faith to imagine there is intelligent life scattered throughout the universe. Many religious people have a hard time believing in evolution and life on other planets, while many atheists have no trouble at all, accepting this as a forgone conclusion. And, indeed, if we consider the size of our known universe, and if we consider a God who is both infinite and eternal, how silly to assume we are alone in our intelligence, and how naïve to think we were not placed here by design and with a perfect purpose in mind.

But what is the purpose of creation, and what is the reason for our existence? Perhaps our purpose is to know God more fully, to gradually become more like him, and to one day be perfect—perfect in love and perfect in goodness. Jesus said, "Be perfect, as your Heavenly Father is perfect." Perhaps now we are mere spiritual infants, but in time we will be fully grown, fully enlightened, and fully entrusted with the secrets of the universe. Perhaps our purpose is to overcome all fear and ignorance. Perhaps our purpose is to be cocreators with God. Perhaps our purpose is to learn to love, respect, and protect one another. Perhaps our purpose is to enjoy each day and discover the good in every living thing.

Our life on Earth is not our only adventure, but it may be one of our most important. This is where it all begins, where the foundation for a future life is laid. This is where we make our evolutionary debut and where God first calls us. This is where we change from being purely animalistic to altruistic. This is where we change from being material minded to spiritual minded. This is where we move from self-centeredness to God-centeredness. This is where we first learn to be loving, kind and caring.

Evolution has brought us this far, but now we must take a step of faith to begin our next stage of evolution—a spiritual evolution. In spiritual infancy, we are often afraid of change, unaware of our own ignorance and unwilling to go where God is leading us. When we become spiritually mature, we have an expanded faith, a larger vision, a greater sense of a divine plan, and we are able to break through to higher levels of living. We advance courageously. We grow in humility. We become more thoughtful and fruitful. When we are spiritually mature, we are able to calm our minds, concentrate on peaceful outcomes, and work to create peaceful spaces for everyone. We are able to show loving-kindness and treat others with dignity and respect. We are able to treat ourselves this way. We are able to realize our role as compassionate caretakers and caregivers and take bold steps toward protecting our planet.

To become mature minded is to realize you have the power to align your thoughts with God's thoughts and your will with God's will. To be spiritually mature is to realize you are not an accident, a prisoner of fate, a slave to the planets and stars, or a victim of circumstances. It means understanding your own inner strength and deciding to work with God, not against him. When you learn to make decisions with God, your life will take on a whole new meaning. By committing to his plan for your life, you will overcome fear and procrastination, gain a sense of purpose, and experience greater freedom. You will begin to bring heaven to mind, heaven into your home, and heaven to Earth.

When you turn to God wholeheartedly, you will naturally surrender to all that is good and true. You will see that you live and move and have your being in God. You will begin to use your time and talents to help others and improve your quality of life. You will use your education and resources to change your way of living and giving. You will use your influence not for selfish gain but to make the world a better place. You will seek happiness not solely through sensual gratification, but through selfless service and spiritual growth. You will courageously rise to meet the challenges and difficulties of life, knowing you are working as one with God.

Many are given visions of things to accomplish or ways to improve themselves and the world, but too often they are put aside in favor of lesser things. The greater thing God would have you do, the truer calling he would have you pursue, is set aside in favor of small pleasures or put off entirely and eventually forgotten. Maybe an idea rises up within you again and again, but it seems unrealistic given your age or lack of experience, time, money, or education. You calculate how you could do the thing you feel called to do, but steps are never taken to bring it to pass. You fear what others may think, so you remain silent. You worry about the effort that will be required of you, so no energy is expended. You hold a limited opinion of yourself, so God's will for you remains only an idea in your mind. As time passes, the vision fades, the impulse to do more lessens, the will weakens, and the dream dies.

If only you had brought your concerns to God. If only you had remembered to have the faith of a child. If only you had asked him to illuminate your path. If only you had asked for the strength, courage, and discipline to pursue his best plan for your life. Instead, the person God would have you become, the work he would have you do, and the adventure he would have you pursue, remain out of reach. The growth he would have you experience never becomes a reality. The action he would have you take and the skills he would have you master are put off and pushed aside due to all manner of little things. We rationalize, worry, compromise, and say we are not able or not ready to obey the vision, when we are ready; we are just not willing.

God would not call us to begin a good work if we were not ready. What is he calling you to do? Are you ready to decide with God rather than against him? Do you sense you should begin something new? Perhaps change your behavior, begin a new career, slow down, speak up, relieve someone's suffering, get out of an unhealthy situation, complete your education, commit to a relationship, or become a parent?

God's callings do not have to be grandiose. Maybe he is calling you to plant a garden, beautify a living space, read to a child, take up pottery, put down your phone, be more patient with your partner or kinder to your kids. Usually, we know what we should be doing, or the direction we should be taking, without anyone telling us. God has planted the seed of who we are to become within us, so deep down we already know. If we procrastinate, God just keeps nudging us, whispering to us, and giving us more and more reasons to choose his way.

When you know you should be doing something but prefer to put it off, it only leads to unnecessary anxiety and delay. What a relief it usually is when you simply choose to act, address the problem, have the conversation, change the habit, begin the project, or do the thing you've been putting off. God wants to help improve not only your life but the lives of everyone around you. So if you find yourself in a place where you have no peace and in a world that's gone mad, ask yourself: What would God have me do?

God would not ask something of you that you could not accomplish. Nor would he ask something of you that would not benefit you and those around you. After all, he is trying to help you bring heaven to Earth and to prepare you for heaven beyond Earth. But don't think that following God's plan for your life will always be easy or predictable. Sometimes, when you are being led in a new direction, it will feel extremely uncomfortable. When you are being led to change your lifestyle, it will seem difficult or even impossible, but if you trust God through the process, in time it will come to feel natural and fitting, and you will acquire a new sense of contentment, satisfaction, and accomplishment.

God's callings can be large or small. They can range from lifelong pursuits to short-term endeavors. They can be within any area of work, within any sector of society. They can result in dramatic breakthroughs or gradual improvements to your well-being. What all successful callings have in common, though, is a relationship based on trust—between the called and the one who calls. God trusts you to grow, to change, to advance, to overcome fear in all of its ugly forms, to love, and to do your part to bring heaven to mind, heaven into your home, and heaven to Earth. But that's only half the equation. You must also trust God to lead you in the right direction, to bless your work, to guide you in all truth, and to safely carry you through eternity.

God speaks to everyone according to their particular personality and temperament, and he works within each person individually. You can have a quiet, private calling that is just as perfect and divine as a notable, public calling. You do not have to be a great orator, run for public office, appear on TV, or win a peace prize to fulfill God's will. You may just need to simplify your life or purify your thoughts. You may need to humble yourself and apologize. You may need to raise your expectations and act. You may need to be less sour and more sweet. You may need to tell others no, in order to restore your sense of peace and balance. God wants us to be free to live original lives. He does not require that we all look alike or think alike in order to be alike spiritually. Every person and personality is different, and God delights in our diversity, but he also delights in our coming together as brothers and sisters. When we manifest love, joy, peace, patience, kindness, goodness, faithfulness, gentleness, and self-control, we are displaying the fruits of his Spirit, actively uniting our world, and bringing heaven to Earth.

You will know someone is close to God's heart not when they call themselves religious, spiritual, Christian, Muslim, Jewish, Hindu, Buddhist, or any other name; not when they are from a certain country or speak a certain language; not when they are wealthy, powerful, or popular; not when they support one political party or economic system over another. You will know they are close to God's heart when they display the fruits of his Spirit and devote themselves to bringing heaven to Earth.

God speaks to us in many ways, but in the end, the message is the same. He calls us to live together on this big blue planet as one family. He calls us to love him, to love one another, and to love all of his diverse creations. This is our true purpose, so why ignore the call? Why put it off in favor of lesser goals? Begin today to live in love. Begin today to ask how you can love yourself more and share your love with others. Begin with whatever time, energy, and resources you have available. Begin with the personality you have been given. Begin with the dreams and desires you have within you. Begin where you are now. Begin with the circle of people God has placed around you. They can sometimes be the most difficult to get along with, but decide to live in harmony with others, to whatever extent is possible. At home, at work, at school, in society, begin to set a positive example for others. Give people a reason to hope and a reason to smile. Be a source of healing and humor. Be a source of strength and security. Be an example to all of gentleness and goodness.

Remember the vastness of our universe and don't take your tiny world too seriously. Remind yourself that God has a perfect plan for us all, and our time on Earth is only one small portion of this overall plan. Spend your time here wisely. Take your work seriously, but try not to take yourself too seriously. It may be helpful to remember that you are not the center of the world, and Earth is not the center of the universe. The universe is beyond what we can fathom; it stretches into infinity, and there is intelligent life throughout that is too vast and diverse to imagine.

Even on this one small planet, there is such an abundance of life and such a variety of species and personalities.

If your worldview has become so small that you are no longer curious, questioning, seeking, reading, serving, connecting, or enjoying life, why not? If you're bogged down in hopeless, negative thinking, you've most certainly lost sight of the big picture. If you think there's nothing more to learn or explore and no one new to befriend, think otherwise. If you're living in your head, start living from your heart. If you're living too much from your heart, try using your head a little more.

Maybe you need God to pull you out of the minutiae of life. Maybe you're stuck in a particular mindset or routine. Ask God to expand your horizons and show you how to transform your world into a more heavenly home. Ask him to help you be less critical of yourself and more forgiving. Ask him to help you be less judgmental of others and more accepting. Ask him to help you be more persistent in the pursuit of your dreams. Ask him to help you dream of peace on earth. These are the small things you can do each day to help make a big difference in your life and the lives of others.

Life can easily wear us down and leave us feeling overwhelmed. Maybe you grew up in a place where you had to overcome many hardships. Maybe the world around you has suddenly changed, and you are doing your best to survive. We all suffer setbacks in life, but not everyone can work through their patches of darkness to reach a point of peace. We all get lost and take wrong turns, but not everyone can correct their course and find the road God would have them travel. Some people are lost so deep in the woods they've stopped asking for directions;

they've given up hope. And some are so turned around they're taking directions from people more lost than themselves. Why wander aimlessly when today you can connect with the one who oversees all paths? Why allow others to remain lost when you can do your part and lead them home?

When we talk to God, we must have faith that he is listening, that he cares, and that he is actively working to improve our lives. When we wake up each day, we must also have faith in ourselves and in our ability to care for our families, earn a living, pursue our dreams, and help bring heaven to Earth. Hundreds of times a day we are called on to exercise our faith—when we go to work, send our children to school, pay our bills, get on a plane, or go to a doctor's office. In each case we are trusting that we will get through this day just fine, that tomorrow will come, and that God has a master plan for our lives. We can never know the full extent of God's grace acting upon us or how all things are working together for our good, but by faith we can accept that they are.

Certainly there's a lot out there to destroy our faith, and if we're not careful, we can easily lose our peace and lose our way. Sometimes we can get so overwhelmed by life that just one wrong word can trigger an avalanche of emotions. Or one small offense can spark a regrettable action. What thoughts are racing through your mind? What is keeping you up at night? Ask God to free you of any dark imaginings. Let today be a turning point. Ask him to help you escape a lifestyle that has you feeling frustrated or depressed. Ask him to show you how to live a more fulfilling life. Ask God how you can gain a sense of belonging. Be sincere, be direct, and then be willing to listen and invite change into your life. Don't ever think your circumstances are permanent. Everything can change tomorrow. Everything will change eventually because nothing is permanent apart from God's unchanging character.

Pause for just a moment, quiet your mind, settle your nerves, and let go of any negative thoughts and emotions that have been building up within you. Acknowledge that your imagination may be playing tricks on you, making your problems appear larger than they actually are. Try countering your negative thoughts with positive, practical ones. Say to yourself: Maybe my situation is not as it seems. Maybe I don't know the whole story of how this will play out. Maybe what I'm thinking isn't true. Maybe things are really bad, but a solution is right around the corner. Maybe tomorrow will be better. Maybe God has already set things into motion for a peaceful outcome. Perhaps those negative voices are wrong. I won't let frustration or fear cripple me and keep me from moving forward. This is temporary; everything is temporary. Something good will come out of this. Even though I'm in a bad situation, I'm growing wiser. Even though this process is painful, I'm getting stronger. God will use this experience for my highest good. It's always darkest before the dawn. I will eventually have a wonderful breakthrough. I don't know what the future holds, but God does, and I trust him. God is working behind the scenes to help me get through this. God is with me even now. Everything is going to be okay.

Begin to trust God as your Heavenly Parent. Know that he loves you and wants what is best for us all. Even though hardships can and will befall us, God can always illuminate our minds and show us the best path forward. Begin today to hand your problems over to God, and then allow him to hand them back to you with solutions attached.

There is a part of you that no eye can see or look upon. It is the part that cannot be clothed, adorned, or known by others. It is the hidden side of yourself that only God can see. It is the quiet, eternal side that is guarded by your Heavenly Father. Just as we learned when we were young not to judge a book by its cover, we must learn again and again not to judge ourselves or others based on outward appearances. We must begin to place a higher value on our inner lives. We must learn to see as God sees, which is the purest form of vision.

When we concern ourselves with popular opinion, we can easily be disappointed. When we value only what the world values, we can become lost. When we focus only on the material side of life, we can get no relief. The world is busy, and it cares little for us. Attitudes change, fashions change, trends change, opinions change, landscapes change, times change. Civilizations rise and fall, leaders come and go, buildings and people are built up and torn down. Today you can be a media darling, the apple of someone's eye, well loved, and highly favored, but tomorrow you can be an outcast. People are fickle, but God is never fickle, and his love for us never falters.

If you want to find peace within, begin to rise above the superficial, competitive, consumer side of life. Begin to exchange the perishable for the imperishable. Begin to let go of old ways of thinking, living, and relating that no longer serve you. Begin to realize you will never find lasting peace apart from God. You are an eternal being, a spiritual being having a human experience, and no amount of human activity will be completely satisfactory, because you are made for something more. You are made to be in relationship with God, and apart from him you will always be searching and hungering for something more.

When you retire from a job, you leave it behind. You clean out your desk and walk away. You say goodbye to old friends, colleagues, and bosses; those you have loved, loathed, and begrudged. You begin a whole new lifestyle. You no longer get up and follow the same daily routine. You stop fighting traffic or wearing work attire. You stop worrying about the deadlines, meetings, goals, and responsibilities that once preoccupied you. Everything comes to a grinding halt, and you are given an opportunity to reinvent yourself. Similarly, just as you can retire from a job, you can also retire from daily habits that wear you down. You can retire from thoughts that leave you paralyzed by anger, fear, or sorrow. You can retire from relationship routines that drain your energy. You can retire from long hours of worry and busyness that leave you no time for spiritual growth.

The end result of spiritual maturity is always peace and joy. When we know we are secure in God's love, we are able to relax and trust where he is leading us. We are able to gain a sense of belonging and self-worth. We are able to shift our priorities to creating caring communities, which will lead to a caring society, which will lead to well-being for all. The first step, though, is deciding to bring heaven to mind. Maybe that means finally accepting that God loves you and wants you to be happy. Maybe that means taking time each day to care for yourself, nourish your body, rest, pray, relax, and reflect. Maybe it means stepping outdoors, going for a walk, or finding a place where you can quietly connect with your Creator. Maybe it means finding refreshment throughout your week, so you won't need to permanently retire from life.

Our world can be challenging, even overwhelming; that is why it's important to check in with God each day. Parents love to hear from their children, and your Heavenly Parent is no different. A few minutes alone with God will help ground you, calm your mind, and remind you how truly loved you are. God wants us to be in fellowship with him, but he also wants us to live in harmony with others. We are all his children, and we are slowly awakening to the truth that we are one global family. So do your part to participate in life, to build friendships, to care for your family, to serve one another, but be careful not to lose your sense of balance. Throughout your day, take time for your Heavenly Father, because when you walk with God, you walk in peace.

Enjoy each day and be thankful for work that takes your mind off your personal problems, focuses your attention, and makes you feel useful, but always save a little time for God. Take pleasure in shopping and clothing your body, but consider your soul, and clothe it too—in mercy, kindness, goodness, and joy. Work hard at school, and enjoy participating in sports, music, and extracurriculars, but make room in your schedule for prayer and reflection. Take pleasure in an active social life, and be thankful for many friends, but consider your Creator, and befriend him, too. Be grateful if you have a comfortable life, but don't live for the world's approval. Don't ever become so entangled with the world that you lose sight of God. Don't become so distracted by all the shiny objects that you settle for fool's gold rather than pure gold. Don't exchange the authentic life God would give you for a cheap imitation.

Maybe in the past you've been too hard on yourself, always comparing yourself to others or judging your life against unrealistic standards and ideals. Ask yourself, how did these ideals develop? What are their roots? Is the lifestyle you aspire to grounded in what God wants for you? How does God want you to live? Are you basing your worth on what others say is worthy? Are you judging your life against the lives of family, friends, neighbors, strangers, or celebrities? Take some time to consider God's opinion of you. What does God consider a successful life? What does God call a beautiful life? What does he want for you? Measure yourself against God's standards. Are you happy? Are you kind? Are you forgiving of yourself and others? Do you have a tender heart? A clean conscience? Are you patient with those around you? Are you doing the best you can? Are you living to make the world a little bit better off?

Jesus said, "What shall it profit a man if he gain the whole world and lose his own soul?" How do you lose your soul? By severing your connection to God and hardening your heart to others. And how do you gain the world while losing your soul? By enriching yourself at the expense of others, putting profits over the well-being of the planet, improving your bottom line while exploiting workers, accumulating wealth while putting untold stress on families, and rising in power and influence while failing to help those in need. Jesus did not warn against hard work or the possession of property, but he did warn against giving preference to material values over spiritual ones. He did not want us spending our days focused on money, power, possessions, and sensual pleasures to the exclusion of love, service, decency, and truth.

Take some time to explore the spiritual side of life. Try to envision all that might be good and pleasing to God. Do you devote part of your day to silence, prayer, reflection, or inner contemplation? God is concerned with your inner person, the one hidden away. He wants to spend time with you and expand your understanding of all that is. He wants to make you aware of his love. He wants to tell you that though you are on a path toward perfection, he does not condemn you for your present imperfections.

Though Jesus instructed us to be perfect, just as our Heavenly Father is perfect, we should not assume God is waiting for us to reach some final point of perfection before he starts loving us. He loved us yesterday, he loves us today, and he will love us forever—just as we are. Becoming more perfect, more purified, more peaceful, more thoughtful, more charitable, more fruitful, is a process that will carry us into eternity. It is not something we can accomplish in one short lifetime on Earth. All God asks is that we do our best each day, that we try, that we have good intentions, that we don't give up, and that we forgive ourselves and others when we fall short of perfection.

Even when we try our best, he knows we will stumble, because the way of perfection is not as we might imagine. It is not an easy, predictable path forward or a linear curve upwards. It is often a rollercoaster ride full of unexpected twists and turns. It is sometimes one step forward, three steps backward, and five steps sideways. It is a journey of faith. It is a lifetime of trusting, praying, risking, failing, trying, quitting, and advancing. It is an invisible path of uncertainty, doubt, loss, struggle, growth, setbacks, and breakthroughs. God is always moving us in the direction of perfection, but his ways are not our ways. His ways are often shrouded in mystery, so the path he has us travel can sometimes seem confusing, dimly lit, and dangerous. Nevertheless, he guides us along the way, and he loves us all the way home.

Do parents withhold their love until their children reach adulthood? Likewise, God does not wait to start loving us until we reach a certain level of maturity or morality. He loves us all the time, at every age, in all situations and through every difficulty. Would a father fault his young child for falling while learning to walk? Likewise, God does not fault you when you try and fall or risk and fail. Would a mother be unresponsive if her child fell while riding a bike and cried out in pain? Likewise, God does not stand at a distance, judging us and ignoring our cries. Rather, he gathers us in his arms, comforts us, and assures us that all is well. He understands each stage of our growth and development, and he is patient and attentive to our needs. He knows that painful experiences are sometimes a natural and necessary part of life. He knows we must pass from the early childhood years, to the elementary years, to the middle school years and beyond. He knows we are a work in progress.

Are you disappointed by life? He would still your mind and reassure you that all is well. He would give you every reason to hope for a brighter tomorrow. He would give you time in your day to sit with him. He would show you the way out of every dark place, if only you would turn to him. If you fall, he will help you stand and try again. If you fail, he will help you regain a sense of confidence and purpose. If you lose your way, he will help bring you back to a place of peace. If you struggle in any area of your life, he is there. Allow him to help you with your relationships, your emotions, your finances, your work, your world, and all that is troubling you. Let him show you a way to once again be happy and whole. Let him help you become the person he knows you can be.

As you develop a relationship with God, you will find that your thinking will begin to shift, your attitudes will soften, your plans will change, and your courage will grow. Gradually, your priorities and ambitions will take a turn for the better, until one day your entire outlook will improve. Before, you were perhaps frustrated, afraid, worried, angry, overworked, without purpose, or in pursuit of dead-end goals, but then you began to consider goals with God in mind. You began to realize the immediate and eternal rewards for those who follow his will. There is peace for the peacemakers, mercy for the merciful, blessings for those who consider the poor, abundance for the diligent, and goodness and gladness for the pure of heart.

Throughout the day, as you reach out to God, let him bring to mind his best for you. Maybe you will be led to become a kinder person—to yourself, your family, friends, people who don't look like you, think like you, vote like you, act like you, or worship like you. Maybe you will decide to choose one person each day to whom you can be kinder, and then you will form a habit. Maybe you will decide to be known for your kindness as well as your hard work, for your good heart as well as your good job, your character as well as your career, or your warmth as well as your wealth.

As God touches your heart and opens your mind, you will naturally begin to bear fruit, the fruit that grows from within and originates with God. You will begin to radiate love and show evidence of joy, peace, patience, kindness, goodness, faithfulness, gentleness, and self-control. When you are in touch with God's Spirit, these fruits will naturally emerge, but not necessarily all at once. That might take some time; for some, a lifetime. We are slowly traversing the universe, so be patient as God pulls you toward perfection. Like a giant magnet, he draws us all out of wrong doing and wrong thinking, to purify us and show us the way of compassion and cooperation.

Chapter 3

Jesus said, "In this world you will have tribulation, but be of good cheer. I have overcome the world." He said this not on a bright, sunny day in Jerusalem, while looking forward to a long life of peace and prosperity. Rather, he spoke these words in the dark of night, in a farewell address to his friends, just prior to being betrayed, humiliated, tortured, and killed. How could he have possibly meant to be of good cheer? That he had overcome the world?

Jesus said these words because he had done a lifetime of work learning to connect to the Divine within. He was in a higher place, a place that allowed him to rise above his circumstances, a place that allowed him to see God in all faces, a place that allowed him to extend mercy and forgiveness to all. Despite misconceptions, false accusations, insults, and acts of violence against him, he knew the truth about himself, and he knew where he was going. He did not identify with the words of his accusers, nor did he stoop to their level to defend himself. He was grounded in goodness, secure in God's love, and confident in his eternal destiny. This allowed him to find peace in the midst of uncertainty and composure in the midst of calamity.

Yes, in this world we will have tribulation, all manner of problems, sometimes trouble on every front and times when we don't think we can make it through, but we have a way to rise above it all. We may not be able to physically escape our circumstances, but we have a way to find peace. We may not be able to walk away from our difficulties, but we have a way to face them with a new attitude. We have a way to make our faith outshine our fears.

Every day will bring its own set of challenges, but we have the ability to be of good cheer. We have the ability to overcome the world. God calls us to live in such a way that defeat, defensiveness, and discouragement will not take root in us. When we seek to connect with God each day, nothing can destroy our peace of mind. When we start to get overwhelmed, when we want to give up, when we begin to take things too personally, all we need to do is stop, take a step back, and share our burdens with the one who can calmly deliver us from the raging storms of life.

Fear is always the greatest storm to be overcome. It may move in gently like a fog, but if left unchecked, it can grow to be a hurricane. It can engulf your life and cause you to react in ways that damage relationships and destroy everything you hold dear. Maybe you have a small fear that causes you to withdraw and dwell more heavily on your problems. Before long, you are imagining a dark chain of events unfolding, your peace of mind is shattered, and you're thinking and acting irrationally. When we magnify our problems and keep fear at the forefront of our thinking, we rarely make wise decisions. We open doors for depression, paranoia, and even violence to enter.

Maybe you are worried about your health or your finances, and this fear gradually morphs into a larger concern about your future or the welfare of your family. You keep your thoughts to yourself, not wanting to upset or disappoint anyone, and soon you are all bottled up and filled with anxiety. You magnify your problems, so they become larger with each passing day. In the privacy of your mind, you create scenarios that paralyze you with fear. You don't ask for help or share what's troubling you, and soon everything is spiraling out of control. You can reverse this tide, if only you will take it to God in prayer. There is no shame in turning to God and others for strength and solutions. There is no shame in asking for help.

When we spend our waking hours only dwelling on our problems, we naturally become more and more anxious. Alone with our thoughts, we draw all sorts of conclusions and visualize all sorts of terrible scenarios. Soon we are filled with terror, and like Jesus's disciples in a boat on the stormy Sea of Galilee, we are shouting out incredulously: "Don't you care about us? Don't you care that we're drowning?" We can't believe that the one who should be saving us is sleeping. Surely the wind and waves will destroy us. We work ourselves into a state of panic, believing the world is indifferent to our pain and oblivious to our cries, when all we need to do is reverse the tide of fear that is engulfing us.

When we are faced with a crisis, it's easy to feel alone and blot out all hope of a positive outcome. How quickly negative thoughts can fill our minds, when all we need to do is breathe, quietly go within, and share our thoughts with God before we are completely overcome by doubt and dread. Just as Jesus calmed the wind and the waves and cast out fear from his troubled disciples, allow God to restore your sense of peace as well. Listen, as he asks you: "Why are you so afraid? Have you no faith?"

Take a few minutes to sit with God. He oversees the entire depth and breadth of creation. Don't you know he watches over you too? He invented time and space and upholds all that dwell within it—giant nebulae, galaxies, solar systems, planets, black holes, and every living thing. Don't you know he upholds you too? Don't you know he loves you? Allow him to give you a reason to hope. Listen as he reminds you to be of good cheer.

When fear and pessimism fill our minds, we lose our ability to think clearly. We are barely able to pray, and less likely to treat ourselves and others with kindness, dignity, and respect. When fear sets in, we are unable to imagine positive outcomes. If, however, in a moment of sanity, we can quiet our minds, God will use that opportunity to share his wisdom and peace. Do you need an answer? A solid piece of advice? A way out of a bad situation? A new way of looking at an old problem? Listen to the voice within. Listen as you are led to a friend or a solution. Sometimes in our quietest moments, when we set ourselves apart from a crowd or awake from a long slumber, when our minds are most at ease, God will reach us and tell us what we need to hear. Listen for those words of wisdom. Listen for a positive, uplifting message to emerge. Listen for guidance and new ideas. They won't come if you are constantly in a state of panic, though. Quiet your mind and trust that you will receive a reassuring word. And if an inspiring thought comes to you and you feel God is leading you to act, be willing to move forward in courage and faith.

When we fear the future, it can be crippling and result in wasted time and wasted resources. It can lay the groundwork for all manner of hardships, including poor health, poverty, crime, addiction, and divorce. On a larger scale, if we have a society filled with fearful citizens, it can pave the way for economic instability and social unrest. Mass hysteria can lead to violence and the creation of innocent victims and scapegoats. We can prevent fear from spreading, though, when we control our individual fears. The responsibility for peace begins within each one of us. If we each do the hard work of taking control of our thought life, calming our minds, connecting with the Divine, and seeking solutions to our problems, the cancerous cells of fear, hostility, and chaos can eventually be eradicated.

When we promote false, divisive ideas, innocent minds can easily be influenced, and people can be persuaded to take wrong action. One voice can quickly become the voice of many, generating a mob mentality and laying the groundwork for conflict and violence. But there is always an alternative, and it's easier than we may think. It is peace with God, peace within ourselves, and peace with our neighbors. It requires a moment of calm and thoughtful consideration of how we would like our lives to unfold. It requires trusting that God's plan can be accomplished peacefully and nonviolently. It requires patience, prayer, honesty, and deep reflection. It requires hitting the pause button before we say or do something we will regret. It requires making compassion and self-control virtues of the highest priority. It requires rising above harsh words and raw emotions in order to see others from God's perspective. It requires setting aside our egos, and sometimes even our instinct for self-preservation, in order to reach out to our enemies, find common ground, and resolve our conflicts peacefully.

Despite our best efforts and our most sincere prayers, however, there is no guarantee that trouble won't find us. Pray as we may, we can still get sick, get into disagreements, grow discouraged, and be overwhelmed by life. Storms can still appear on the horizon, and problems can pop up all around the world. Pandemics can overtake us, floods and droughts can displace us, heat waves and wildfires can engulf us, wars and tragedies can befall us, and politics and any number of issues can divide us. There is a guarantee, however, that no matter what we face, God will be with us through it all, and in due time he will bring us out.

But even when our days are calm and all is well around us, we should not become complacent. We should dare to stretch our faith, venture to do more and expect more from life. We should ask God every day how we can help bring heaven to Earth. God wants to extend his love through you. He wants to help you become a force for good. He wants to help you overcome the limited thinking and personal prejudices that may be holding you back. He wants to help you dissolve your resistance to positive, constructive change. He wants to do something larger in your life. Pray that God will help you make the right choices along your path, and then trust him to have the perfect plans, people, and places all lined up for you.

At all times God wants us to be free, but he knows that sometimes too much freedom can lead to wrong choices. Therefore, he offers his gifts in increments, in order to protect us. He would have us grow to be free both within and without. He would have us become free from all unnecessary hardships, free from bad habits and wrong living, free from harmful routines, small-mindedness, painful secrets, and thoughts of a dreadful tomorrow. He would also have us be free of all political, economic, and religious systems that mislead, enslave, and diminish us.

If life becomes unbearable for a majority of citizens, we must ask ourselves what role we are playing in either the uplifting or degradation of society. What are we doing to bring about positive change? What are we doing to simplify our lives and improve the quality of life for others? What are we doing to help make our fellow humans happier, healthier, more secure, and less desperate? What are we doing to lower the temperature of the world? What are we doing to ensure a more equitable distribution of wealth? What are we doing to preserve and share the world's resources?

Doing your part to transform the world may mean changing your routine. It may mean being less plugged in, spending quality time with loved ones, or taking quiet walks outdoors so new attitudes and ideas can emerge. It may mean becoming more plugged in, joining conversations online, or sacrificing your time to help solve a problem facing your community or the world. If you think the problems of our world are too complex and unsolvable, think again, and consider the genius of your Creator. Maybe something that seems impossible to resolve just requires a little more patience and persistence. If you are just awakening to the problems facing our world and the ways you can make a difference, don't give up—on God, on others, on yourself, on hope. In time, all things will be made lovely and new.

There are small things each of us can do every day to make life more enjoyable for all. Where we've sown discord, we can work to sow peace. Where we've been selfish, we can remember we're part of one global family. Where we've been cold and calculating, we can strive to be humble and humane. Where we've embraced division and intolerance, we can work to bring about harmony. Where we've been indifferent, we can learn to be of service. Where we've been part of the problem, we can resolve to be part of the solution. We can tone down the rhetoric, lower our voices, turn away from divisive talk, open our minds, listen, and respond with patience and kindness.

Every day you wake up, challenge yourself to be kinder—to the kind and the unkind alike. Make kindness your default setting. Be an example for others to follow. Be an inspiration to someone who has not felt kindness flow toward them in a long, long time. Smile. Be of good cheer. Do your part to clear the air and prevent toxic environments in your home, office, school, community, and country.

And let's not forget to be kind to our planet, Mother Earth. For centuries, we've asked so much from her, taken so much, and given so little in return. As a mother, she's spoiled us, but now she is aging, and we see how our selfishness has hurt her. We've used her to advance and enrich ourselves, but in the process, we have destroyed her beautiful landscapes; stripped her forests; mined her mountains; polluted her air; paved over her meadows; poisoned her streams, rivers, and oceans; ravaged her jungles; harmed her wilderness; and caused too many plants, animals, and people to suffer and die.

Have you ever stood at the ocean's edge and enjoyed a beautiful sunset or sunrise? Have you ever walked on a beach, played in the surf, or ridden the waves? Have you seen whales breach in the distance or dolphins frolic nearby? Have you seen a turtle emerge from the water to lay her eggs on a sandy shore? Have you been snorkeling or scuba diving around a coral reef? Have you looked down on the ocean from an airplane window? Have you lived a fisherman's life? Or felt the delight of being at sea? Take a moment and fondly remember these times, and say a prayer of thanks for the oceans God has given us. God chose the oceans as the incubators of life. It is where we all began, but today they are slowly dying, even while continuing to nurture, inspire, and sustain us.

Year after year, the oceans have quietly borne the brunt of our misguided choices, but now they are hurting and crying out. Because they are so vast, we have taken them for granted and assumed they would remain self-sustaining and unchanging. But now they are showing us how vulnerable and interconnected we both are. As the oceans absorb the excess heat from our environment, they kindly buy us time to reduce our greenhouse gases and make wiser choices. But they cannot absorb our pollution and excessive heat forever and go on living without evidence of pain. In time they show their scars. In time they express themselves the only way they can—by giving us fewer ice sheets, fewer coral reefs, less ocean life, rising sea levels, more flooding, more powerful hurricanes, more heat waves and cold waves, and more droughts, all of which makes less fresh water available, puts enormous stress on all living things and pushes many species to extinction.

The level of carbon dioxide in our atmosphere has not been seen in several million years, and soon we might surpass a level not seen in one hundred million years. It's time for us to all look in the mirror and recognize the role we play in either helping or hurting our planet. With self-reflection will come insight, and with insight will come greater compassion. We will begin to see the full price we are paying to live in a society that places a heavy emphasis on consumerism and materialism. And with God's help, we will begin to open ourselves to new ideas, new inventions, and new ways of thinking and behaving.

It is good to extend your kindness to your family and those in your immediate surroundings, but now we must extend it to all of mankind, all of nature, all of life. We can no longer take clean air, clean water, and hospitable ecosystems for granted, ignore the problems at hand, and expect future generations to clean up after us. We must start now and work within our own spheres of influence to make a positive difference. Maybe it's recycling, redesigning packaging, using biodegradable plastic, eating less seafood, giving up meat, consuming less dairy, installing solar panels, using less fossil fuel, flying less, becoming more informed, voting for candidates who support a peaceful coexistence with nature, supporting businesses that encourage the welfare of workers and animals, donating to charities that help protect the environment, growing local gardens, planting trees, reading books on global warming, watching documentaries about our planet, or developing a greater appreciation for the beauty of our world.

You may live in a comfortable home surrounded by trees, with access to parks and clean air and water, but not everyone does. Do not think that just because your life is nice, no one is suffering. You may one day be a minority. In your lifetime, you may see entire islands and cities wiped out by rising sea levels. You may see the mass migration of people seeking refuge from flooded or drought-stricken areas. You may see large parts of the world transformed into inhospitable habitats, which will affect you, your children, and grandchildren. Therefore, seek God's advice on what you can do now for our world. When you have a determined spirit and a caring heart, you will naturally do the right thing.

In God's eyes, greatness and goodness cannot be separated. You cannot be one without the other. God measures our growth according to the development of our character. He would have us become good before we can become great. He would have us reflect the way of heaven. Are you at peace within, even in the presence of your enemies? Then know you are mirroring heaven. Are you honest and trustworthy? Then know you will be given greater opportunities to advance. Can you tame your tongue, even in trying times? Then know God is watching and will richly reward you. Are you able to serve your fellow human beings, particularly those in greatest need? Then know you will be considered great in the eyes of God and the angels. Have you mastered the art of hospitality? Then know your home will be filled with love and laughter. Do you show yourself friendly to the kind and unkind alike? Then know you will have many friends and admirers. Do you promote justice for all? Then know you are doing God's will. Do you show mercy and understanding, even to the guilty? Then know God will show mercy to you.

Jesus said, "He who would be greatest among you, let him be servant to all." The rewards for your unselfish service, kindness, and generosity are great, with some to be realized in this life and some deferred until the next. The guardians of our universe look out upon all the worlds of time and space, see the progress of all intelligent beings, know the thoughts, motives, and intentions of all, wait for our greatness and goodness to evolve, and rejoice as we gradually become Godlike.

People once thought of God as a judge and a taskmaster, but Jesus showed us the true nature of God. By his words and example, he gave us a broader understanding of God, one that emphasizes love, mercy, fairness, peace, and cooperation above all else. In the Old Testament, the prophets emphasized the sternness of God and the importance of a strict morality. Laws were laid down, and people were expected to follow them. We still have laws, and God still calls us to righteous living, but he accounts for our weaknesses.

Jesus helped focus our attention on the love our Heavenly Father has for us and the love we should have for one another. He ushered in a new way of living and relating. He helped us look beyond all that would make us feel hopeless, trapped, weak, small, or ashamed. He taught us to believe that with God all things are possible. He helped us measure our self-worth not by what others say, but by what God says.

Jesus taught a timeless message. He spoke not only to those of long ago, but to every person, of every nation, of every age. He spoke of the remarkable love of God, and the great need to love one another. He spoke of a lifestyle to transcend all worry, selfishness, hatred, and fear. He spoke of a way of life filled with compassion and unplagued by stinginess and small-mindedness. He spoke of the need to be as wise as serpents but as harmless as doves. He spoke of the importance of justice, fairness, and mercy. He spoke of how our lives can be filled with a deep sense of calm, peace, security, and joy.

Jesus taught us a way to be happy which runs contrary to our modern pursuits of happiness. Today we seek happiness in many forms, from shopping to skiing to spending time on social media, but Jesus taught that we could find happiness in unselfish service, in showing kindness, in being a peacemaker, and in ministering to those in distress. He taught that being humble and merciful could bring happiness. He said, "Happy are the pure in heart, for they shall see God." He even taught that being persecuted in the brave pursuit of goodness and fairness can bring happiness.

Jesus said, "Happy are the poor in spirit." Yet this runs so counter to our belief that happiness comes from the accumulation of wealth and from an increase in power and possessions. The poor in spirit are those who are humble, those who have been dealt several life blows, who have known heartache and seen suffering. They are no longer boastful or think of themselves as self-made, self-important, and self-sufficient. Rather, they are teachable, open to the truth, and more willing to seek spiritual goals over financial or material ones. The poor in spirit have laid down their egos and decided to cooperate with God and be gently led by him.

Jesus taught that we are to be the salt of the earth and the light of the world. We are to add flavor, spice, and everything nice to the world. We are to add hope, humor, peace, and understanding. We are to love our enemies, do good to those who hate us, bless those who curse us, and pray for those who spitefully use us. And yes, as we do all this, we can be happy.

How is this possible? It is possible when we slow down the pace of our lives and decide to see the best in others. It is possible when we see our enemies not as enemies at all but as members of an extended family. It is possible when we talk, listen, and seek to humanize one another. It is possible when we develop the habit of being kind, honest, and helpful, rather than critical, suspicious, and condemning. It is possible when we forgive. It is possible when we understand all the factors that contribute to violence, desperation, and mental illness and then work to bring about solutions to these problems.

Albert Einstein once said the most important question we can ask ourselves is whether the universe is friendly. Nearly two thousand years before Einstein asked this, Jesus went about answering it. He taught that yes, indeed, our universe is friendly, that it was created by a loving God, and that it is perfectly upheld and administered. He taught that God is the loving overseer of our souls and the giver of life. He taught that within all people there is a part of God, his Spirit, which grants us free access to his mind and an understanding of his thoughts. He taught that though our bodies will one day die, we will live forever.

Jesus taught not only through stories, parables, and instruction, but by his example as a God-filled person. He lived simply and was a learned man; a fearless man; a good, morally upright, optimistic man. He was a man with a strong, magnetic personality. He was meek in that he submitted himself to God's will, but he was not weak by any means. He feared no one, despite the brutality of others toward him. He loved little children, the poor, the sick, the lost, and all those who searched for truth and a better way of life. He understood people; he sympathized with them, appealed to them, healed them, and devoted his life to uplifting not only those of his generation but those of future generations who might pause to consider his message.

And what was the message he most wanted to share? What is the message that stretches over two thousand years into our busy twenty-first-century lives? It is not a message about political parties or economic systems. It is a simple message about true religion, a religion that focuses on personal spiritual experience. Jesus was not interested in institutions. He was interested in individuals. He was interested in improving our inner lives, which he knew would then improve our outer circumstances, which in turn would uplift society as a whole. He worked from the inside out to bring about change. He built up people's faith, connected them to God, educated them about God's will, and put them on a path for better living.

He offered an appealing religion of personal transformation, which was free of force, formalities, rituals, and strict rules of conduct. He taught that by connecting to God, we can display the fruits of God's Spirit—love, joy, peace, patience, kindness, gentleness, goodness, faithfulness, and self-control. As we increasingly take on these Godlike qualities, we naturally become better people, partners, and parents. We become better citizens who can then go out into the world to bring about positive change, improve our institutions, and help create heaven on Earth.

Jesus taught peace on earth and goodwill to all people. He taught the importance of a genuine and sincere faith. He taught that by simply believing, rather than following any formal rules of religion, one could enter an invisible kingdom governed not by an actual king or a strict ruler or a recordkeeper of sinful acts, but by a Heavenly Father who loves us.

Take a moment to consider Jesus's message of two millennia ago. What he offered his followers then and what he offers you today in our modern world are the same. Are you the least bit overwhelmed by life? Reach out and take the hand of God. Allow God's Spirit to flood your heart and mind. Allow yourself to be born anew. It won't cost you a penny, only a little time, a quiet prayer, and a sincere heart. God's love and transforming power are free gifts to you, but you must be willing to claim them. You must have the faith of a child and boldly take hold of these priceless packages. Take a moment and ask God for a peace that passes all understanding. Believe you can have a life of freedom and joyful service. Close your eyes and ask to live in a friendly universe. Then open your eyes and know you are already there.

Chapter 4

Do you wish to know more about your Creator? Then listen to the wind and the waves. Let the ocean and sky tell you an ancient story. Allow Earth's creatures to reveal the kindness and nobility of God, and let the trees become your windows to heaven.

Consider the majestic southern live oak tree, how it stretches tall and wide, bringing shade to all those beneath its canopy. It is long-lived and strong, providing food and shelter to those in its care. Though its branches bend and twist from time and weather, it becomes more beautiful with each passing year. Other trees may shed their leaves and go dormant in the winter, but the live oak remains verdant and watchful. It is a tower of strength, a place of refuge where the weary can go to find rest for their souls.

Just as a seed grows quietly in the soil and a young tree grows slowly on the lawn, so too does God grow in our minds. Gradually, the tree will mature, our view of God will evolve, and the landscape within and without will change. At the appointed time, we will see the tree in all of its glory, and we will come to know God in all of his goodness, and we will love them both all the more.

Do you wish to know more about your Creator? Then look to the ocean, how it surrounds and sustains us. How it gives us oxygen, food, beauty, serenity, recreation, jobs, marine life, even carbon-capturing whales to help regulate our climate. How it connects us to nature and improves our well-being. How it exists between us, yet binds us together as one global family. How it is vast and expansive, yet searchable. How it is powerful, yet approachable. How it is mysterious, yet familiar.

The ocean can be cold, dark, turbulent, and terrifying, or warm, clear, calm, and inviting. It depends on your perspective. It can fill us with fear or bring us delight. It can be the source of hurricanes, shifting sands, sharks, and tsunamis, or a sea of tranquility, a refreshing reservoir, a blue heaven. It depends on your perspective. It can be a dormant beast, suddenly rising from great depths to inflict injury on the innocent, or it can be a big friendly giant, happily greeting us at the shore. It can move in swiftly and violently or gently lap our feet at its edges. It can rain down terror or leave us undisturbed. It depends on your perspective. It can push away boundaries and uproot lives or it can respect our need for privacy and safe spaces. It can stir up storms and behave erratically or it can reassure us with its steady, rhythmic tides. It can demand our last breath as it pulls us downward or it can grant us new life, becoming a gateway to heaven. It depends on your perspective.

The ocean will prove itself faithful if you will allow it. It will show itself predictable if you get to know it. It will warn you if you listen. It will grant you safe passage, protect you in its harbors, feed you, console you, and fill you with a sense of wonder, if you can trust it. It will ebb and flow and deliver up endless messages if you take the time to learn its language. It will change form, depth, and direction, but it will never leave you or forsake you. It will bear all things, endure all things, and forever remind you of the goodness and grandeur of God.

There is a gentleness within nature, not unlike God's Spirit, that can become your teacher. But you must take some time to consider the flora and fauna. You must learn their language, for they have so much to say. Pause now and then and allow nature to share her wisdom with you. Take yourself to the seaside or countryside. Find time to enjoy the great outdoors, to wander in the woods, and to seek out rivers, creeks, and pastures. Go in search of a sliver of land, a park, a garden, a yard, or a tree-lined street to explore. Spend a morning, an afternoon, or an evening with nature, listening and learning. Give yourself permission to walk, lie down, wade in, swim, and befriend all that surrounds you. Try slipping your shoes off. Try planting your feet in the soil or burying them in the sand. Begin to trust the one who governs the universe. Begin to live in partnership with God. Accept his call to unite our troubled world. Accept his call to extend kindness to all.

To understand God's character, his care and protection, it helps to spend time in nature, but it also helps to have a tender affection for the most vulnerable among us. It helps to have experienced selflessly providing for a child, a pet, an elderly parent, or someone who is sick—loving them, bearing with them, listening to them, and encouraging them. When you take on the role of parent, teacher, or caregiver, you quickly begin to understand God's great love for us. For what is parenting, teaching, and caregiving? It is a shift from selfishness to selflessness. It is a new beginning. It is the high calling of life. It is an education in empathy, kindness, humility, patience, and tolerance. It is a mirror showing us the sides of ourselves we never knew. It is the giving away of ourselves, the sharing of our souls, and an awakening to love. It is the wondrous, all-consuming, life-transforming experience of serving those most in need. It is preparation for heaven.

There is a continuous ebb and flow to life, which we must accept. We draw others close and then gradually release them. We bathe in their affections and then watch as they run off to play. We cradle them and coach them and then allow them to make their own way. We devote ourselves to their care, do the best that we can, and then they are gone. Loving and caring for others can be immensely rewarding but also exhausting. It can lift us up with joy and bring us down with worry. It can fill us to overflowing with dreams of a bright future and then taunt us with thoughts of a dark tomorrow. It can splinter our hopes with doubt. It can age us. It can make life worth living and then remind us of the brevity of being.

Raising children can bend us, sometimes break us, but always put us together again stronger than before. If we are rigid, children will teach us the art of flexibility. If we hold grudges, they will educate us in forgiveness. If we expect too much, they will give us the gift of dashed dreams and disappointments so we may learn the lesson of unconditional love. Yes, children are often our wisest teachers. Under their tutelage, we learn to take the good with the bad, to roll with the punches, to give up judgments, to surrender to laughter, and to gain a new perspective on life. When we see through their eyes, we learn to see what is truly important. What was once meaningful can become insignificant, and what was business as usual can seem unmindful, uncaring, and unkind.

We learn empathy when we see our children struggling to live up to our expectations. We learn compassion when their real lives become reel life, with all of its adventure, comedy, drama, mystery, romance, and sometimes even horror. We learn patience when they forget the good times and magnify the tough times. We learn steadfastness when they make mountains out of molehills, and we bring them down to size. We learn self-control when they become junior courtroom lawyers, arguing and objecting to sound advice and instruction.

When our children are young, they are completely dependent upon us. The sacrifices we make may be great, but we are richly rewarded for our efforts with hugs, kisses, singing, and laughter. Despite any episodes of fussing and fighting, there are sweet displays of tenderness and affection that soon follow. But as children grow, they naturally become more self-sufficient and independent, and sometimes we struggle to stay connected. By the time they are teenagers, we are often trying to bridge two separate worlds. We have our world of work and responsibilities, and they have their world of school, social media, sports, activities, and friends. Sometimes all we want is for them to turn off their technology and talk.

To begin to get a taste of God's approach toward parenting, imagine the very best your parents offered you, combined with the affections and creativity of your favorite teacher, the kindness of a beloved relative, the patience of all the saints, and the highest wisdom and understanding of all parents throughout the ages. Then multiply that by an infinite amount, and you will have God's approach to us. While we're usually patient, he is consistently and infinitely so. While we're sometimes selfless, he gives of himself throughout all eternity. While we're generous on occasion, his very essence is generosity. He is removed from all that is miserly, fearful, selfish, questionable, or unkind. Despite all that he witnesses at each stage of our growth and development, God never tires of loving us. He never tires of connecting and communicating with us.

It's really not a great mystery, the nature of God. He loves us like a devoted parent. He wants the best for us. He wants to spend time with us. He wants us to experience his presence, acknowledge him, put down our devices, and start a conversation. He wants a one-on-one relationship. He is not an impersonal, mechanical God. He is not a distant entity or a remote energy field. God has an actual personality, and his goodness can be known. But too often, like sullen teenagers, we give him the cold shoulder. Maybe we make an initial attempt to acknowledge him or reach out to him, but then we become distracted or disappointed. We end up ignoring him, struggling to relate to him, misunderstanding him, taking him for granted, or becoming indifferent to his presence.

But God is not human. He will never become frustrated or exhausted by our behavior. He will never abandon us when we abandon him. When we rebel or grow cold, he will not count it against us. When we slip up, he will not give up. When we are slow as sloths to learn our lessons, we will be no less adorable in his eyes. He does not judge us for our perceived shortcomings. Rather, he builds our character on all that we consider mistakes and failures. He takes our painful experiences and turns them into something beautiful and transformative. He gives meaning to our lives and endlessly guides us in the direction of freedom and peace.

His Spirit moves continuously within us to show us a better way. He endures all things with patience and grace. When we push him away, he reaches out to connect. When we rush full steam ahead in the wrong direction, he corrects our course. When we completely forget him, he moves to awaken us. He gives us flashes of insight and opens our eyes to the beauty and inequity of our world. He pours forth his goodness and has us return to love, again and again.

God gives us free will, knowing full well how self-seeking, stubborn, irrational, insensitive, and even violent this may cause us to be. God harbors no base thoughts and has no reason to fear our ability to think and act independently. He did not design us as automatons, because he is no mere programmer of life. Nor is he an autocrat, but a loving Heavenly Father who has placed his Spirit within us so that we may know the fullness of life and have access to his very thoughts. God trusts us to think, to choose, to plan, to learn from our experiences, and to find our way in a difficult world. He sets boundaries for our growth, but he gives us great swaths of time and space in which to roam and grow. The path he has placed us on, whichever way we may turn, will always lead to him. It is only a matter of time.

Within God's eternal plans, he has factored in our choices, limitations, and struggles. He sees all the events of our lives at once. He sees the obstacles confronting our parents and ancestors before us. He sees us from conception through to the grave. He sees all of the joys and sorrows of each life. He sees humanity slowly transforming Earth into a more heavenly home. He sees us departing Earth and adventuring through the heavens. He sees every sun, moon, and planet, all the way to the outer edges of the universe. His vision knows no boundaries. He is eternally focused on all that is good, beautiful, and true. He sees the best in us, at all times, in every circumstance, for all of eternity.

God is generous and gives, but we should not confuse his generosity with that of Santa Claus at Christmastime. Santa gives freely to us as children, asking nothing in return, and God does as much and more, but his gifts are everlasting and indestructible. You will never have to hand God a list of things you think will make your life bearable and complete; he knows what you need even before you ask. God cares about your material welfare, but he also cares about who you are becoming. So when you quiet your mind and pray, don't ask for more stuff; ask instead that your life be simplified so you may find peace.

God won't magically make your dream car appear in the driveway or a new wardrobe appear in your closet, but he can help you find a better way of living if you seek to connect with him. He can help you advance and overcome obstacles that might hinder your progress. He can help you become more resilient and determined in the pursuit of your goals. He can help you become more content with what you have and more focused on your true calling. He can help you manage your money so you are less anxious about tomorrow. He can help you manage your time so you can become more accomplished. He can help you become more confident so you can find your true voice. He can help you know true happiness and acceptance. He can raise you up despite the doubts of others and help you succeed against all odds. He can stir up your faith, open doors of opportunity, expand your vision, propel you forward, clear your path, point you in the right direction, and encourage you to keep going, keep hoping, keep trying. He can help you see yourself less through the world's eyes and more through his eyes. He can help you move safely through this harsh, competitive world until you find your way. He can help you find rest in him each and every day.

God's gifts come from a different realm. He does not fill our stockings with toys but fills our hearts with love and our minds with truth. And when we beg for material blessings, it may appear as though he does not hear or care, but indeed he does. He just cares far more about perfecting our character and advancing our souls. He cares that we awaken. He cares that we work to make life more peaceful and pleasant for all. He cares that we hold fast to our faith and not give up—on ourselves, each other, and dreams of a better tomorrow. He cares that we learn to control our anger, passions, and egos so heaven is not prevented from breaking into our lives. He cares that we not remain stuck at the same level of learning, where we repeat our mistakes again and again, never maturing, never improving, never gaining the knowledge, power, and momentum to overcome small, imprisoning lives.

But even in our imprisonment, brokenness, and complacency, when we have failed to learn our lessons, God is there, and he would say: Choose again. Choose a better way. Choose to keep going, to forgive, to be good. Choose to let go of selfish pride, but learn to think more highly of yourself. Remember you are a child of God, and choose to act with integrity. Choose not to be paralyzed by fear. Choose to smile. Choose to be kind. Choose to recognize that God is working all things out for your highest good. You may not know the exact outcome of events or what tomorrow will bring, but God does, and you can trust him. Let him lead you out of all hardship to a place of peace.

Learning to trust God is the easiest thing you will ever do and the hardest. It's easy because you are simply reaching out to your Creator, in the quietness of your mind, and inviting him into your life. It's the most natural thing in the world. But maintaining a relationship with your Heavenly Father and choosing again and again to stay connected requires a commitment. We are surrounded by so many distractions that can pull us away from God's guidance, and we are faced with so many temptations that can lead us in the wrong direction and cause us to wander aimlessly. But even when we wander, God loves us no less. He watches over the lost, bleating sheep and the happy, faithful flock as though they are the same. He loves us all equally, and in the end, he gathers us all together as one.

The shepherd will certainly come for you when you stray, but why wander and put yourself in harm's way? Why leave the flock, where you can be safe and secure? When sheep go astray, they can easily become lost, drown, fall over a cliff, or be attacked by wolves. When we go through life like wayward sheep, we are inviting unnecessary pain, isolation, and danger. But if we remain with the flock, we are protected and under the watchful care of the shepherd.

Staying with the flock requires a decision to stay connected to God throughout the day. It means realizing the power within you and the strength of community. It means making choices to display the fruits of God's Spirit—love, joy, peace, patience, kindness, gentleness, goodness, faithfulness, and self-control. It means becoming a more disciplined thinker. We often form mental habits that do not serve us well, so we must become aware of negative thought patterns. We must guard against all that would cause us to become fearful, troubled, and isolated.

We must remember the important people in our lives and choose to stay connected. We must remember God and share our problems and concerns with him.

Perhaps you have formed a habit of worry; it's your favorite pastime. If you watch the news regularly, you know there's a lot to worry about. We're often given the impression the world is coming to an end. Too much news can leave us feeling anxious about the future, the environment, the economy, our health, and our safety. But we can control the way we feel. We can control what we watch. We can control what we think, and we can begin to deflect all of the anxious thoughts pressing in on us. With an awareness of God, we can form new ways of reacting to events. We can face bad news and bad reports without losing hope. We can develop a deeper sense of calm, knowing God upholds all things. We can remind ourselves that God is in control and there are invisible forces at work behind the scenes. We can remember that the universe is friendly, that there are solutions aplenty to our problems, and that God will aid and enlighten us in becoming problem solvers.

Perhaps all you need some days is to take a break from the news to calm your nerves. Consider it a vacation from a major source of sadness and anxiety in your life. Try spending some of the time you would normally spend catching up on the news, catching up with family, friends, or God. Try a new routine. Try doing one thing differently that will help bring heaven to mind, heaven into your home, and heaven to Earth. Try stilling your mind and allowing yourself to experience the peace that passes all understanding.

Throughout the day, if anxious thoughts begin to fill your mind, try treating them like paper airplanes. When they come flying at you, be quick to swat them away. Imagine a room full of little boys making paper airplanes and throwing them in your direction. What troubling thoughts are swirling overhead? Catch them in midair, wad them up, and throw them in the wastebasket. Don't let them bother you. Don't let them break you. Every airplane may represent a serious problem, but for now, swat them away and consider it a game. Rather than getting overwhelmed and annoyed, try to lighten up and play along. Trust that God has a solution for each and every problem.

Give a name to every plane that comes your way. Give one the name of a difficult relationship you may be having, another the name of a health concern, another the name of a bill you don't know how you'll pay, and another the name of a more substantial problem or crisis. Whatever is agitating you and circling overhead, knock it to the ground. Exercise your faith and trust God to help you overcome it. Then go chase those boys outside. Send them out to play, and reclaim your peace. Don't allow negative thoughts to permanently invade the sacred space of your mind. Reconnect with the Spirit within, and listen for a whisper of hope, a word of healing, a reminder to smile. Listen for a way out of a bad situation, for guidance, for a revelation and answers to your problems. Listen for the sounds of children laughing in the distance.

It's easy to get discouraged by people and events that seem to conspire against us, but remember, we are all moving in the direction of perfection. We are growing, learning, becoming, and expanding our awareness of all that is. If you lack riches, if you have enemies, if you are overwhelmed by your surroundings, or if you are disadvantaged in any way, don't think that God is punishing you. Remember, we must learn to see through his eyes.

We must learn to take the long view. God may be using your circumstances to purify and perfect you and those around you. He may be setting you up for a future success of which you are unaware. He may be transforming the world through you into something more beautiful. He may be working within you right now, bringing fruit to life and heaven to Earth.

God knows what each of us is capable of handling, and he knows when too much of anything may lead us down the wrong path. We all want to win the lottery. Maybe the lottery you're hoping for is one of fabulous wealth, perfect health, gorgeous looks, a dream vacation, an amazing relationship, a happy family, or easy living, but the true lottery to be won is knowing God and becoming more like him. Maybe your present discomfort is because you think a door has closed when God is actually trying to move you in a new direction. Maybe the misfortune weighing you down is a gift in disguise, one which God will use to refine you, strengthen you, and prepare you for a higher calling, both in this world and in the world to come. You are here on Earth for such a short while, so why not use your time wisely to grow your soul? Why not have a little faith and patience as he helps you see your life, your relationships, your country, your world, even the whole universe with a new set of eyes?

God has great plans for us, and this does not involve having us spend our days in misery and despair. He wants us to be clothed in joy, strength, and dignity. But we each have lessons to learn about compassion and community. We each have callings to fulfill and people to care for. We each have negative attitudes that must be rooted out. We each have seasons of struggle, which we must pass through. We each have moments of testing before we can be given a larger vision for our lives. We each have trials to endure before we can know a better way of living and relating. Experience moves us all in the direction of perfection, but make no mistake, none of us is perfect yet. We all still struggle. We all grow tired and lose our way. We all make mistakes and suffer humiliations. We all push boundaries and face disappointments. We all dare and suffer defeat. We all strive to improve our circumstances and enlarge our lives. We all wish for more happiness, peace, prosperity, freedom, acceptance, and love. But to get there, to have all that we so desire, we must be willing to grow, change, listen, and learn.

Just as we can learn other languages—Arabic, Bengali, Chinese, Dutch, English, Farsi, French, German, Hebrew, Hindi, Italian, Japanese, Korean, Portuguese, Russian, Spanish, Swahili, Turkish, Urdu, Vietnamese, and so many others—we can also learn the language of Spirit. But how can we discern the voice of God? How can we know if Spirit is speaking or if we're just mumbling to ourselves? Fooling ourselves? How can we know definitively when the Divine is trying to get our attention? In a word, peace. When Spirit speaks, you will have an inner sense of peace. You will know that what is said is both true and good. God's guidance will never leave you feeling unclean or uneasy. His ways are simple, loving, clear and profound.

Maybe you will have a quiet knowingness, a small epiphany, a moment of serendipity or a flash of inspiration. Listen often to this guidance, for God speaks to us in many ways. He is always present, and always leading us in a more perfect way. When God touches you and opens your eyes, you will understand more clearly what he is calling you to do. You will have a newfound energy and desire to improve yourself and the lives of others. You will turn away from needless distractions and become more fully focused on his will for your life. And day by day you will be led in the way you should go.

Take time every day to quiet your mind and listen. The voice of Spirit is soft, gentle, and kind. It is never harsh, loud, or condemning. It is a voice that gives you quiet insights and leads you to wiser choices and more excellent outcomes. It is a voice that leads you to become more compassionate, courageous, and caring. It is the voice that says, Be patient but persistent in your efforts to improve yourself and effect change. It is the voice that says, Expect more from some people but less from others. It is the voice that saves you from disappointment. It is the voice that cautions you in your criticisms. It is the voice that guides you to keep going but encourages you to rest. It is the voice of balance, reason, and tender affection.

God is just as concerned that you take care of yourself as he is that you help improve the world. He cares about your well-being. He would have you slow down if you are too busy. He would have you nourish yourself if you are ignoring your body's basic needs. He would have you pray and exercise your faith rather than worry. He would have you believe that you don't have to fix all the broken people in your life. He would help you solve a problem that is causing you frustration. He would help you change your attitude or repair a relationship if you have lost your sense of peace. He would help you grow in compassion if you are being unkind. He would have you trust that his guidance is available to you at all times.

Each life is a book, and starting today you can turn the pages of your life and begin a fresh new chapter. Imagine waking up each day to dialogue with the one who knows you completely, loves you unconditionally, and longs to lead you down the most perfect path you can hope to walk. The path is perfect because God designed it for you. The path is rewarding because it offers every good thing to bring you into a greater awareness of love, beauty, and truth. The path is difficult because you will want to stray but will be brought back. The path is friendly because it will bring you into greater fellowship with your brothers and sisters. The path is essential because you must go from this life to the next.

Imagine a beam of light stretching all the way from God in Paradise to you on Earth. From the heart of God to your heart. From the mind of God to your mind. From God's home to your home. There is always that connection, always that indwelling Spirit, always that opportunity to tune in to the Creator of our vast universe for lasting comfort and peace within. When God made you, he made you with an everlasting umbilical cord. It connects you to your Heavenly Parent, it nourishes you, and it aids you in your growth. You are eternally connected, but this is hidden from your human eyes. You must take it all on faith.

You will never be able to prove that God lives within you. You cannot measure, observe, or provide empirical evidence regarding the existence of God. No scientist will win a Nobel Prize for proving the reality of God. Believing in God is an act of faith. It is the first step, but an enormous step, in the long journey toward trusting God and becoming more like him. It is a great leap forward from spiritual infancy to maturity. It is a recognition, at last, of the intelligent design of our universe. It is an awakening to the loving governance of the cosmos. It is the realization of the untapped power and potential within us. It is the understanding of things to come. It is the substance of things hoped for but not seen. It is your entry ticket to the game of advanced living.

Imagine going through life not knowing the reality of who you are. It's like a child of royalty being put up for adoption at a young age and then having to go through life in abuse and squalor. Year after year your past grows more distant until eventually all you have is a faint remembrance, somewhere deep within, of who you were. Something instinctively tells you that you are more than your circumstances. Your outer surroundings don't align with the way you feel on the inside. You have an irrepressible sense that you were meant for something more, have the potential to do more and be more, to shine brighter and be happier...if only. If only what? If only you could know the truth. If only you could know your Heavenly Father. If only you could see your original birth certificate and reclaim your heritage.

Bridging the gap between what we inwardly sense and outwardly observe must begin with a step of faith. By faith you must accept you are more than the name you were given and more than the person you see in the mirror. By faith you must accept you are someone special who is always emerging. By faith you must trust the small voice within. Just as the whisper waits to become a roar and the seed waits to become an oak tree, so does your dream of a better day wait to become a reality.

We all have the capacity to dream, and God is no different. Before God created the universe, he dreamed. He dreamed of a limitless playground made of time, space, energy, and matter. He dreamed of an abundance of life. He dreamed of spiritual and material realities. He dreamed of heaven and Earth. He dreamed of an expanding universe and an untold number of galaxies. He dreamed of his love stretched out upon an endless network of living creatures. He dreamed of the infinite advancement of beauty and truth. He dreamed of perfection arising from imperfection.

He dreamed of unity within diversity. He dreamed of a loving relationship with all.

Even before we were born, God's dreams for us were vast, varied, and original. He dreamed we could start out small, just ooze in saltwater, and eventually grow to be Godlike. He dreamed we could ascend from plasma to animal to human to angelic. He dreamed we could go from selfish to altruistic. He dreamed we could grow from mortal to immortal. He dreamed we could go from simple to complex and from unaware to fully conscious. He dreamed we could go from dwelling in briny waters, to trees, to caves, to soaring skyscrapers, to heavenly homes. He dreamed we could come to fully appreciate not only food, water, air, sex, and shelter, but also art, beauty, fellowship, love, laughter, music, nature, philosophy, science, wisdom, and worship. He dreamed we could overcome all manner of harsh environments and threats to our existence—ice ages, droughts, fires, famines, disease, earthquakes, global warming, hurricanes, violence, and wars—to bear fruit, even spiritual fruit. He dreamed we could learn to administer our affairs wisely, care for our planet, love one another, and live in peace. He dreamed we could overcome all vestiges of mean-spiritedness and small-mindedness to one day experience joy, kindness, and cooperation. He dreamed we could grow to love him, even as he loves us.

God's love is simple and profound, vast, and infinite. Nothing in all of creation can separate you from the love of God. It is everywhere. It is within and without, just waiting to be discovered. If you feel alone, as though no one sees you or cares for you, know you are only mistaken. You are only briefly unaware of the immense and ever-present love of your Creator. Just a small shift, and you will be brought into the warmth of God's all-embracing love. It is a hair's breadth away. Ask God today for an outpouring of his love and fatherly affection, and receive whatever your heart will allow—whether a few drops, a light rain, a small shower, or an endless flow of his tender mercy.

A parent's love is a supreme love. It makes room for mercy. It allows you to love through difficult times. It allows you to respond selflessly, overlook small offenses, and offer correction without harsh consequences. It allows you to respond without fear, anger, or intimidation. It allows you to return good for evil. None of us would be here were it not for the loving example set by others in our lives, and none of us would have the capacity to love were it not for the work of God's Spirit within us. We are all shaped both from within and without, as we slowly become more perfect vessels.

The highest concept we can have of God is a Heavenly Parent, but sometimes it may help to think of him as a Potter. As such, he places us on a potter's wheel, where he molds us and sometimes painfully transforms us from soft clay to lasting works of art. He shapes us into chosen vessels, covers us with beautiful glazes, places us in a kiln, and then brings us out as new creations. Every piece brought forth is unique, perhaps a simple bowl to be used at suppertime, an exquisite vase, a colorful platter, or a raku teacup. Like pieces of pottery, when we finally emerge from the fiery trials of life, we too will be transformed, beautified, and given new lives of loving service.

God is a Master Artist who once imagined our entire universe, called it forth, and gave it life. Now he continuously dedicates himself to his art, refining his creation and perfecting the lives of his children scattered throughout time and space. He takes us in his hands, shapes us, and allows us to be placed in the kilns of life so that we can come forth more excellent than before. He abides with us as we withstand the tests of time to become the poised, purified, and enduring works of art he envisioned. When at last we are presented, we will appear as power cloaked in compassion and purpose wrapped in longsuffering. We will be the beautiful vessels he intended, able to contain all that is lovely and true, and we will pour forth his blessings upon all living things.

Chapter 5

When you train your mind to focus on God's goodness, you will begin to recognize this same goodness within you and within all living things. Spending time with God will lead to peace within, while running from him will only lead to wasted time, unfruitful endeavors, and unnecessary sorrows. So begin today to work with your inner tutor, who wishes to bring you to complete spiritual maturity. Do not be content learning your ABCs when God wants to help you advance beyond a kindergarten curriculum. Choose to cooperate with your Creator so you may gain a clear vision for your life and become a blessing to those around you. When you devote yourself to discovering and doing God's will, you are one step closer to experiencing a more perfect world where all may know God's complete provision and peace. Why wait another day?

When we begin to trust God and rely on the inner workings of Spirit, we can take a great leap forward as individuals and as a society. We can gain a larger view of life—of our purpose in this world and in the worlds to come. We can realize we are all part of a global family, as well as part of a broader cosmic community, which will gradually unfold to us. We can be mindful of our unique roles and prevent ourselves and others from becoming cancerous cells that infect the whole body. Each day we can do our part to bring heaven to mind, heaven into our homes, and heaven to Earth.

By spending time in silence each day, we can allow the sweet Spirit of God to rub off on us. When we are in the presence of greatness, we can't help but feel better and make better choices. So if you have been avoiding God or if you have been weighed down by fear or frustration, it's time for a change. Welcome a new season into your life. Stop thinking of God as a remote, heartless being. Though the universe bends toward justice, God is not a judge or a law enforcer; he is our Heavenly Father. As such, he endlessly empowers us, patiently corrects us, and mercifully forgives us. He does not sit on a throne shaking his finger at us. He does not disapprove of us from a distance. He does not curse or condemn us. He made us the way we are, and he knows we are a work in progress. His desire is for us to feel loved, safe, peaceful, happy, and free. He knows planet Earth is a difficult place to live, and he does not stand in judgment of us.

God created us as imperfect beings, yet designed us from the beginning to grow toward perfection. He formed us to evolve, create, overcome obstacles, solve problems, uncover mysteries, and advance. He made us so that we learn through trials, errors, mistakes, and failures. He made us so that we gain wisdom through some of life's most difficult experiences. He made us so that we become easily dissatisfied by circumstances that rob us of liberty, deny us the truth, or condemn us to undignified living.

So if you feel you've lived a difficult or disappointing life, fallen short of the demands of family or friends, failed to live up to society's expectations, or become disillusioned by life, go easy on yourself. You are just as God intended you to be, and in due time you will be made perfect, if for no other reason than God himself is perfect.

When we make mistakes, we should remember God's kindness and likewise be kind to ourselves and others. When we feel like giving up, we should remember God's patience and be patient as well. We should remember that God delights in seeing us grow in wisdom, grace, and goodness, but he is in no hurry. He is not disappointed by any lack of progress. He rests knowing the work he does in us is complete. Like a seed containing a flowering cherry tree, you are already that which you wish to be, and in due time everything good and beautiful will be drawn out.

Be patient with your progress, and if you should find yourself criticized or condemned, remember there can be harsh critics and consequences on Earth, but only relief in heaven, as God is not human. We are not asked to befriend a petty god, so ponder this about your Heavenly Father: He calls us to be merciful because he is a witness to our imperfections. He welcomes impartiality because there is nothing unfair within him. He desires sincerity because it is the essence of his being. He promotes creativity because he is the Creator of all things. He admires ingenuity and dedication to one's craft because he is the Master Craftsman. He values the sublime because he dwells in the heavenly realms. He encourages freedom of expression because he lives to share his goodness and truth. He relishes kindness because he is eternally kindhearted. He instills laughter because he is the author of the highest humor. He encourages the gift of music because he first poured forth sound. He fosters our respect because he is respectful of all living things.

God is eternal and infinite. He was not born, and he does not die. He has always been, and he is present everywhere, at once, throughout the universe. Though a part of God dwells within us, there is a great gap of mystery that separates us from all that he is. So while we can draw near to God and he can dwell within us, we should not attempt to make him wholly human. We should not abandon our sense of awe and wonder about our Creator or turn all of religion into a list of laws that must be followed. We should not dull down the Divine by emphasizing strict rules of behavior to the exclusion of all else. We should not create a one-dimensional image of God.

Why do many people dislike organized religion? Because often it is lessons in behavior, when what is needed are reminders of the beauty and fragility of life. Often it is an invitation into cold, institutional settings, when what is needed are warm communities in which we can experience God's love. Often it is an education in the ancient prophets, when what is needed are modern, hope-filled messages. Often it is a cumbersome concoction of traditions, rituals, and doctrine, when what is needed is the simple truth. Often it is barren landscapes, when what are needed are fertile breeding grounds from which personal spiritual experiences can spring.

Why would anyone seek God wholeheartedly when we fail to speak of his goodness and grandeur? When conversations are limited exclusively to the evils of society or the immorality of individuals, we miss the mark, and we lose generations who might otherwise come to know a larger, more profound, more merciful God. The people who refuse to darken the door of a church, mosque, synagogue, or temple sometimes have it right; they instinctively know that God is more than what the religious institutions are presenting. The Sprit speaks to them from within, and it offers a sense, even if ever so vague, that a harsh, intolerant God is to be shunned; a joyless God is to be questioned; a God who discriminates is to be refuted, and a God who cares nothing about you, your family or your well-being is to be avoided.

Some know God in their minds but have yet to feel his presence. Some speak eloquently of God but don't allow him to shine through their lives. Some recite holy scriptures but can't hear his voice. Some are recognized as authorities on God but do not enter into his rest. Some load people down with heavy burdens and moral demands but never lift a finger to help them. Some give sermons on God's will but fail to understand it for themselves. Some know God as a concept but have yet to know him personally. Some approach the truth, standing at its very door, but fail to cross the threshold.

If we wish to be close to God's heart, we must strive to show ourselves as God truly is. We must involve ourselves in the lives of others through loving service and acts of kindness rather than repel them with critical words or indifference to their suffering. We must prove ourselves friendly while providing concrete solutions to their problems. We must make it a priority to refresh and uplift weary souls. We must offer tangible relief from the heavy burdens of life. We must draw people to what is beautiful and true, like bees to sweet-tasting nectar, rather than turn them away and make God nothing more than a bitter pill to swallow.

Instead of always talking, we must know when to be quiet and helpful. Instead of condemning those in the darkness, we must strive to bring them the light.

If we hope to genuinely connect with God, we must come to know the real deal and not a caricature, not the mini-God version. The God we will all love and long for must be a greater and more gracious version than what is often presented. The true God is magnetic and energetic. He is all-loving, all-powerful, all-embracing, all-encompassing, and ever so dependable; there is nothing repulsive about the real God. So if we are to see a God who guides us toward perfection, we must also see a God who does not judge us along the way. If we are to see a God of law and order, we must also see a God of mercy. If we are to see a God who desires right-mindedness, we must also see a God who desires kindheartedness. If we are to see a God who grants us eternal life, we must also see a God who is not indifferent to this life here. We must come to know God as he truly is—One who loves us unconditionally, gives of himself endlessly, and transforms us continuously.

If we are to see a God who corrects, we must also see a God who keeps us from being bound and blind. God corrects us to protect us, because he knows the dangers of perfect freedom combined with imperfect behavior. He rights our wrongs so we can become good, for in our goodness, we can finally know peace and enjoy the privileges he has in store for us.

As much as we need to learn certain lessons here on Earth, we should never relate to God as a strict teacher or taskmaster. He is our Heavenly Parent, and as such, he does more than instruct, correct, and give tests. God forgives us when we fall short, throws out bad grades, tutors us privately, and shows us his tender mercies. He loves us like a devoted parent, with a love which will follow us for all of eternity. He helps us with our studies again and again when we fail to understand. He maintains high standards but overlooks lackluster efforts, never embarrasses or belittles, and patiently encourages us ever more. He takes us out for ice cream because he likes to see us happy as well as wise. He takes us to the park because he likes to see us play as well as work. He takes us to the movies because he likes to see us laugh as well as learn.

Though he wishes to refine us, he is aware of our weaknesses. He is mindful of all the personal, educational, political, social, economic, and physical handicaps that have stunted our growth and weighed so heavily upon us. He is attentive to every act of injustice and every disadvantage we have suffered. So when you struggle through difficult days, know that you are not alone. But know more still. Know that the one who walks with you also bends down to lift you up. Know that the one who holds your hand also upholds the entire far-flung universe. Know that the one who lives within you will remain with you beyond your brief sojourn on Earth. Know that the one who smiles upon you will be gracious to you throughout all eternity.

To be gracious and kind is to be like God. Don't think you lack power to change the world. Your kindness matters. Each day you wake up and choose kindness over impatience, kindness over intolerance, kindness over gossip, hostility, or revenge, you are changing the world. If everyone were kinder to themselves and to others, there would be healthier citizens, happier homes, and more peaceful living. One by one, as we grow kinder together, we will soon reach a tipping point, which will produce dramatic shifts in society. There will be fewer tax dollars spent on weapons, wars, prisons, and police forces. There will be fewer divorces, arguments, accidents, and lawsuits. There will be fewer cases of violence, neglect, and abuse. There will be fewer people trapped in poverty, despair, addiction, and mental illness. Imagine if we lived in a world like that. It's possible.

The Buddha once said, "A generous heart, kind speech, and a life of service and compassion are the things which renew humanity." To be generous of heart and kind of speech requires a connection to the Divine. How easily mean-spiritedness would fall away if we took time to meditate, pray, and attune ourselves to the Presence within. How easily fear, worry, and paranoia would disappear if we believed a loving Creator was watching over us and working everything out for our highest good. How easily we could be kind to ourselves and others if we chose a loving thought over an unkind one.

Kindness requires getting to know others as we ourselves wish to be known. It requires understanding the inner life and longings of others. It requires examining the monsters beneath the surface of our lives, taming those beasts, and not allowing them to provoke us in ways we will regret. Kindness requires leaning on God for help. When you act in ways that are unloving, God asks that you forgive yourself—whether ten times or a thousand times—and try again. He whispers to keep going, keep improving, and keep the goal of loving-kindness foremost in your mind. He helps you close the gap between his thoughts and your thoughts. He helps you overlook an offense and soften your approach to others. He helps you walk a mile in someone else's shoes to gain a sense of empathy. He helps you love the unlovely.

If we knew the loving Spirit that lived within us all, we would be more accepting of ourselves and more agreeable with others.

We would not judge ourselves so harshly or be so critical of those around us. We would consider everyone equal, knowing God loves them as much as he loves us. We would not look down on those who voice different opinions. We might disagree with them, but we would not think less of them. Nor would we judge others based on appearances or anything that would define them externally, because we would recognize God within them. We would seek to bring about harmony by focusing on what we have in common. We would listen more and trust more, and we would no longer persist in unkind ways.

Unlike God, we can never know the thoughts and motivations of everyone we encounter. We cannot know the details of someone's past or all of the circumstances that influence their decisions and actions. We can do an internet search to learn more about someone, but there is a vast difference between what Google can tell us and what God knows. God's understanding of every person is unlimited. He has a complete record of our DNA, family history, thoughts, intentions, words, and deeds. He knows all who have touched our lives and influenced us for better or for worse. And in knowing us so completely, he has complete compassion toward us.

Our knowledge of others, however, is partial and incomplete, so we are far less sympathetic and understanding of our fellow humans. We don't always see the reasons why people behave certain ways. We don't see the history of events, how one thing leads to another, and how upbringing, environment, heredity, and life circumstances may have impacted a person. Therefore, the conclusions we draw are often false, and the justice we demand is often harsh. Because we lack the full picture of a person's life, we offer sharp criticisms and consequences without the necessary kindness and correction.

God has allowed us the free will to form our laws, create our justice system, set up our courts, and build our prisons, but there are higher laws that surround us, which provide a more perfect blend of justice and grace. In the heavenly realms, there is pardon for the sinner, understanding for the wayward, compassionate correction for the wrongdoers, transformation for the depraved, and unconditional love for all.

In asking us to be merciful on Earth, God is not asking us to be lawless or oblivious to evil. He is not asking that we lack the courage or initiative needed to maintain an orderly society. He does not want us to be indifferent to wrongdoing, but he does want us to be different toward wrongdoers. When we are in touch with the Spirit within, we cannot help but think and behave differently. We naturally begin to develop a God-like manner. We take on divine qualities and begin to see others through God's eyes. We devote ourselves to more perfect solutions to life's problems. We advance heaven on Earth, by mixing mercy with justice to bring about fairness.

God calls us to be a peaceful people, but he does not call us to be passive. He does not ask that we suffer harm without asserting ourselves. He does not ask that we remain quiet as others actively seek to take advantage of us. He does not ask that we sit idly by and resign ourselves to undignified living. No, he asks that we awaken, that we express ourselves courageously, and when faced with unjust situations, that we do not merely resist, but that we actively turn the tide—that we become a powerful, positive force for good.

Working to improve society and bring about justice takes time, dedication, and perseverance. We should do our best to bring about positive change, but at some point, we must ask God to help us rise above the battlefields of life. We must turn to God each day, release our heavy burdens, and return to a state of peace. Time may seem cruel, justice slow, and enemies free to roam, but nothing escapes God's notice. Even though God remains eternally compassionate, all acts of injustice will eventually be corrected. Therefore, we should avoid trying to play the role of judge, jury, and executioner, as revenge is never ours. Don't be afraid to stand up for justice, but give God room to move. Trust that in the end, all things will be made right.

Find time each day to quiet your mind. Begin to exchange painful thoughts for more beautiful ones. Know that God wants you to be free, and he wants to help you lay down any negative thoughts or painful feelings that are dominating your life. Even if you think your feelings are justified given your circumstances, at some point you must decide you are greater than your feelings. Remind yourself every day that God wants more for you. He wants you to be internally, externally, and eternally free. You are a child of God traversing this universe, and you were created to advance. Your story is not over.

The strongest power at your disposal, apart from God's Spirit dwelling within you, is your own personal willpower. God gave you the power to choose, to think, to act, and to overcome any negative emotions that are holding you back. You have the ability to discipline your thoughts, make sound decisions, imagine positive outcomes, activate your faith, act decisively, rise above limitations, and take control of your life. As a strong-willed person, you can go far, very far, but you can also go in the wrong direction. That is why you must commit to joining your will with God's will for the best possible outcome for your life. It is only in partnering with God that you can be wholly transformed, lead a truly fulfilling life, and be a blessing to others.

In making your decision to partner with God, you will be given a clear vision for your life. You will have a new purpose for living. Within you will grow the power to change your environment and overcome any obstacles that are holding you back. God wants you to become Godlike. He wants you to be filled with a calm courage, a determined spirit, a strong mind, and a kind heart. He wants to use you as an instrument of peace, joy, hope, wisdom, and change.

God is trying to connect with us at all times to reveal his love and to keep us from beating ourselves up for past mistakes and shortcomings. He would like to rid us of our inner bully—that constant critic who is blind to the good, pure, and lovely—and have us become attuned to the sweet voice within. He would like to win over our hearts and minds until we finally trust him. He would like us to know at all times that when we ask for guidance, it will be given; when we seek more meaningful lives, it will be granted; and when we partner with him, we will be led out of all sorrow into more peaceful living.

So how can we do this? How can we partner with God? The easiest, quickest route out of hell and into heaven is to follow someone who has gone before and successfully overcome all temptation—all thoughts and actions that go against God's will. Jesus is such an example. He had perfect faith in God, and this faith led to an in-depth understanding of his place in the world and his life's mission. It led to oneness with God.

During his time on Earth, Jesus progressed from living an everyday life to taking on his divine nature and reaching the highest levels of religious experience. He understood that he was completely and unequivocally cared for by his Heavenly Father, and he found rest in this reality. He accepted God's good and perfect will for his life, and he felt no need to defend himself.

Jesus is often made an object of worship, with emphasis given to his divinity, but his struggle as a man made him who he is. He chose that struggle, wanting to share in the human experience, and he showed us what can be accomplished in one short lifetime. Jesus wanted people to think more highly of themselves, to realize their infinite worth in God's eyes, and to think of God as a Loving Parent. He wanted us to connect with the Spirit within, to trust in the positive outcome of life, to conquer fear through extraordinary faith, and to spend life in service to others. He showed us how to find complete security in God's love, how to share this love with the world, and how to live with an inner sense of joy and peace.

You too can learn to rest in the arms of God and experience his presence each and every day. You too can allow the will of God to steadily unfold in your life. You too can promote truth and overcome evil with good. You too can bring about positive change on Earth and do great works. When we are led by the Spirit, we can rise to new heights, allow unconditional love to surface in our lives, give up the constant need for self-protection, and learn to experience a life that is richer and fuller than we might imagine.

God is love, and the sprit that comes to dwell within us comes from God. Jesus showed us the highest human experience of connecting to God. He knew God, he walked with God, he had an undivided fellowship with God. He knew what it meant to love and be loved. Love brings out everything good in the human soul. Love heals, uplifts, renews, and fills us with a profound sense of security. Jesus had this love within him that came from a deep connection with his Heavenly Father, and you too can have this love. You can experience this love whether or not you had a parent, spouse, partner, pet, friend, or child who loved you deeply. God loves you, and that is sufficient. God lives within you, and that is the miracle. He can help you conquer all fear, warm your heart, calm your mind, and light a spark within you that will never die.

Reach out today for God's hand. Take hold of it. Trust that your Heavenly Parent is real, living, and actively seeking to connect with you. Let go of your old way of living and begin a new life filled with purpose and divine security. Mark this day, so that in looking back, you can say: This is the day I took hold of God's hand. This is the day I decided to trust that our universe is friendly, orderly, and lovingly administered. This is the day I found rest and was born anew.

Chapter 6

As we grow older, we begin to see patterns, both in the world and in our personal lives. We begin to understand the cycles of life, the way in which life ebbs and flows. We realize how our thoughts, decisions, and actions have consequences. We realize how each season of life is different, yet similar. Life doesn't come with a playbook, so we learn as we go. We take risks, make mistakes, seek advice, search within, stretch our faith and do our best to figure things out. We try, fall, get back up, and then we're off again to experience more that life has to offer.

And life certainly has a lot to offer. It is never static, even when we do our best to lead uneventful lives. Even when we are devoted to dull routines, life has a way of surprising us. Maybe you plan to go about your day in a predictable way, when something as small as a trip to the grocery store changes everything. Maybe a phone call brings you unexpected news, a flat tire has you meet your future spouse, an epiphany has you consider a life change, or a beautiful vista offers you a deeper appreciation for life.

Change is constant within our world, and even though we often resist it, we should learn to go where God's Spirit is leading us, because at all times he is attempting to move us in the direction of life, liberty, peace, and compassion. He is helping us bring heaven to mind, heaven into our homes, and heaven to Earth, but he needs our cooperation. We must be willing participants in this divine dream and be open to the subtleties of Spirit. We must be ready to listen as God speaks to us from within and without—through thoughts, people, and circumstances—and guides us in the way we should go.

Sometimes the changes you need to make may seem too difficult or demanding. Even if you're mildly miserable, you may prefer your familiar habits and surroundings to something new. Being comfortable in the wrong routines, though, can stifle your growth and keep you living a small, shallow existence. It can leave you empty on the inside and defending a lifestyle that is not in your best interest. God wants to help us work through all of the negative emotions and unhealthy habits that are holding us back, both as individuals and as a society. He wants to help us push through seasons of doubt and discomfort until we finally reach a place of greater goodness.

We are all creatures of habit, and we generally prefer our days to be predictable and stress free. Even little changes to our routines can sometimes throw us off balance. Maybe you're out of coffee or diapers at home, your car doesn't start, the internet goes out, a pipe bursts, a pet needs an emergency trip to the vet, or something doesn't go as planned. This can all trigger anxiety in our lives. On a larger scale, maybe your school shuts down due to a pandemic, you lose your job, you experience a family crisis, you end up in the hospital, or you need to move out of your home. Any one of those events can easily pull you out of your comfort zone and leave you wondering how you'll cope. Or consider the birth of a child. It is a joyous, blessed occasion, but it is also a season of change when parents are thrust into a new way of living and relating. There are added responsibilities, less sleep, and more stress. It is the beginning of a new era of increased financial demands, escalating emotions, and untold sacrifices on behalf of your family. It is a season of life that requires flexibility, patience, faith, and humor.

If we can learn to trust God through the changes of our lives, both great and small, we can eliminate a great deal of worry and find peace sooner than later. Change will always be on the horizon because God has planned the universe around our growth and upward progression. Until heaven has permanently settled around us, there will always be unwelcome change to deal with, problems to solve, and stress to overcome. Dark times and fiery trials will come, but they are not the end; they are precursors to breakthroughs in living. They are opportunities to awaken us and help us transform our world into something more beautiful.

Allow God to speak to you from within. Allow yourself to be open to any small change that might improve the quality of living for yourself, others, and all of God's creations. What small thing is God asking you to consider? Maybe he would like you to spend more time listening to someone who needs to be heard. Maybe he would like you to take a day off from technology to tune in to nature. Maybe he would like you to call a friend, write in a journal, or join a support group to help you get through a difficult season. Maybe he would like you to simplify your life so you can be free of unwanted anxiety and tension.

Begin today to become conscious of your daily thoughts, attitudes, and activities. Ask God how you can live a fuller, calmer, happier life. Even if you don't think you need to make any changes, maybe those around you could offer a different perspective. Is there any loving voice you should pay attention to? Is there any voice of reason trying to speak to you that you continue to ignore? Have you pushed people away because you refuse to hear their suggestions or heartfelt concerns? Decide today you will be trusting, flexible and open-minded. Decide you are surrounded by friends and not enemies. Decide you will do one thing differently that will help bring you one step closer to peace within.

People will come and go in our lives, but God's Spirit remains, and each day it calls to us and seeks to guide us in the direction we should go. Each day it attempts to break through the noise of our lives and remind us how much we are loved. God wants you to live a peaceful, satisfying life, but you must have a receptive heart. You must feel you are deserving of love and joy, as are all sentient beings. You must begin to get a sense of the vastness of the universe, the generosity of God, and the transforming power of his Spirit. God loves us and is forever helping us find our way out of this harsh, cruel, imprisoning world. He is helping us discover a more heavenly way of living and relating.

God reaches out to us in every age to help us eliminate harmful traditions, limiting beliefs, and ingrained prejudices that leave us living in darkness and ignorance. He wants to help us change our perception of reality and our perception of one another. He wants to bring us together as one family. He wants to guide us out of fear into caring communities.

If you've been holding on to restrictive thoughts and routines that are not allowing you to grow, expect God to soon lead you out of the small world you've built around yourself. When we stop growing and being in loving relationship with one another, we gradually lose our joy and lose our way. So before you reach that point, where a significant correction may be required, pay attention to the Spirit within, and be on the lookout for any new experiences God may be calling you to embrace. At first, you may be resistant to change, but if God is leading you to move out of a comfort zone, you can trust that the Creator of the universe knows what he's doing.

Choosing to doubt God is like a child doubting his mother as she leads him away from oncoming traffic. God will never lead you in the wrong direction. He will never create circumstances that lead to prolonged stress, stagnation, or suffering. These circumstances are man-made, and they are changeable and preventable. Yet God can be found in the midst of them. He can use any painful condition or troubling situation to get our attention, awaken our minds, soften our hearts, and move us one step closer to heaven.

God knows we have a long way to go in establishing heaven on Earth, but he is persistently leading us in that direction. So if you are stuck in a place of discontent, know that God wants to help move you to a place of greater freedom and peace of mind. If you feel called to do something new, rather than grow anxious or refuse to consider change, try calming yourself and trusting that God is working everything out for your highest good.

Every time we make a choice to follow where God is leading, we are one step closer to experiencing heaven. Every time we are helping build a civil, compassionate society, we are moving in the right direction and winning at the game of life. Imagine a game of chess where you can predict the outcome based on the moves you make. Every move will lead to a different outcome, and such is the game we play. God knows exactly how our lives will turn out based on the choices we make. He knows our thoughts, desires, intentions, and the outcomes of all scenarios. Nothing is too complex for him, and nothing escapes his attention. We have his Spirit as our wise counselor. He's with us at all times to help us make the best choices possible that will move us in the direction of heaven on Earth, but we must be willing to trust him.

God can help you take care of the details of your life, guard your heart, keep you safe in the midst of storms, and provide for your every need. So begin today to trust him, even when you cannot see the outcome of your situation. Even when you are afraid. Even when you are stubbornly resistant. Even when you don't have the smallest inkling of where to go and what to do. Pray for clarity, pray for courage, and then expect him to give you the insight and resolve to advance. Sometimes it's hard to know if you're on the road he would have you travel. You may feel called in a certain direction, but then you give in to doubt. You question the route you're traveling. You look for road signs up ahead, wonder whether you should turn back, and then finally exit the highway. You end up in a parking lot, not knowing what to do or where to turn. Then you wonder what went wrong, but nothing's wrong at all. You're simply human, and as such, you're prone to question, second-guess, and evaluate your progress.

Your destination has not changed, but your confidence in your Creator has. Therefore, when you end up in the parking lots of life, questioning your choices and feeling overwhelmed by negative thoughts, know that all you need to do is calm your mind and turn to God. Give him the little time he needs to rebuild your faith, restore your joy, and return you to the road he has paved for you.

The road we travel, our spiritual journey through time and space, is God's way of teaching us faith, hope, and love. Time is God's measured plan for unifying the universe and helping us realize we are all one. As time passes, the more Godlike we become, the more we take on a Christ-consciousness and the more we are able to create a heavenly home here on Earth.

God sees us on our road trips, and he sees us in the parking lots of life. He sees where we've taken wrong turns and are struggling to get back on course, and if we take time to tune in to the calm voice within, a way forth will be provided. Yes, God works in mysterious ways, but he also works in ways that are obvious and practical. At just the right time, he can bring someone into your life to provide the exact guidance needed. He can cause them to miraculously intersect with your life to get you through a rough patch and inspire you to keep going.

The help God sends you may be an elderly person who has overcome many hardships, has learned the importance of patience and faith, and can teach you valuable life lessons. We should all know people who are examples of quiet strength, wisdom, and dignity. They shine a little brighter than their surroundings and show us how to overcome fear with faith. We never know whom God will bring us in our moments of need. You may not even want to befriend the individuals God is sending you, but if he has caused your lives to intersect, you do not want to ignore the divine connection. Maybe you are old and they are young, you are Muslim and they are Christian, you are black and they are white, you are extroverted and they are introverted, you are liberal and they are conservative. Maybe you are human, and they are of another species. Sometimes animals can be our best friends. It is worth letting your guard down and learning to trust those whom God places in your path. Because it is in our willingness to trust and accept each other that we are made perfect.

To come together, to become unified on our little planet, we must be willing to look into the eyes of those we keep at bay or look down upon or overlook entirely, and say, "I think we can be friends. Despite our differences, I'd like to get to know you. I'm willing to make myself available and listen. I'm going to do my best not to judge you or walk away. I want to hear your stories. I want to know what makes you happy and the burdens you may be bearing alone."

How wonderful it can be when we show some curiosity and compassion, when we decide to let our defenses down, open up, and discover the inner lives of those we may have categorized as strange, different, ignorant, or dangerous. How wonderful it can be to join in relationship with others to have our horizons expanded, our prejudices shattered, our fears dissolved, and our minds put at ease. How wonderful it can feel to be less critical and more accepting. How wonderful it is when we broaden our circle of friends.

A little curiosity can go a long way to getting to know our neighbors on Earth. As we crisscross the globe from city to city or country to country, let us be fair and open-minded. Let us not prejudge one another as we cross boarders or travel from heartland to suburb to inner city. Evolution designed us to be cautious about our surroundings and suspicious of those who are different, but now more than ever before, we must evolve spiritually and learn to come together as a global community. We must learn to work well and play well with others because our survival depends on it.

Getting rid of our prejudices and refraining from labeling others as strange or scary won't be easy. Maybe for you it's people who are a different skin tone or those who listen to different music, live in the shadows, or speak a different language. Maybe it's the poor, the disabled, the elderly, or inquisitive children. Sometimes we're not even conscious of those we're treating differently. It will take time, but once we realize our prejudices, we can take steps to root them out. God calls us to love one another, and when we begin to see each other as equals, we are one step closer to perfection and one step closer to heaven on Earth.

It may take generations, but we will get there. One day we will see all of humanity, all living things, as God sees us—through loving eyes. We will learn to get along, to make decisions peacefully, to be tolerant of those unlike ourselves, and to do no harm to others. The way may seem long and progress slow, but eventually we will come together as one global family, because unity in diversity is God's plan for the universe.

In prior centuries, when slavery was openly practiced, men, women, and children were taken from Africa, shackled and stacked side by side in the belly of ships, and delivered against their wills to foreign lands. Upon their arrival, if they survived, they were bought and sold like goods at a market. They were never considered fully human, so their thoughts, feelings, and well-being did not matter. Their need for warmth, security, kindness, family, companionship, rest, relaxation, education, and freedom was irrelevant to their captors. If they resisted enslavement or tried to assert their God-given rights, they were broken and beaten into submission or killed. This was common practice in many parts of the world for centuries, until we finally awakened to the horrors of slavery.

What is common in our society today that might horrify future generations? Where are we not extending sympathy and kindness to other humans? To other living things? How are we exploiting the world's resources, wrecking ecosystems, wiping out vast areas of wilderness and wildlife, and killing animals to satisfy our cravings? What jobs are causing workers to perform work that desensitizes them to violence, hardens them psychologically, and deadens their consciences? Whose pain are we deaf, dumb, and blind to? How are we overconsuming, taking others for granted, and treating nature as though it cannot feel or express itself? What will they say of us hundreds of years from now? What will they write in the history books?

As God enlightens each new generation, we gradually become more awakened and mindful. We learn the importance of raising the quality of life for all and eliminating harmful ways of living and relating. We realize more fully how everything we think, do, say, and eat ripples outwards. We begin to see that we are not individual islands unto ourselves, but part of one planet, one universe, one creation.

As each generation awakens, we begin to ask ourselves how we can make a positive difference and how we can make Earth a more heavenly home. What more can we do? If the seas are being overfished, can we eat less seafood for a time? Can we pause for a season or a lifetime to allow marine life to rest? If meat industries can no longer feed our expanding population, can we eat less meat or refrain altogether? Can we acknowledge the abject cruelty of slaughterhouses and factory farms? Can we awaken to how other species live, die, and serve us? Can we recognize the side of ourselves that is ignorant and indifferent? Can we appreciate how nature nurtures us and the great need to live in harmony with all things?

If you are going to eat meat, at least become educated in the lives of the animals that feed you. If you are going to consume fish, become aware of the industries that harvest the oceans. If you are going to buy fruits and vegetables at the supermarket, become aware of the business of agriculture, the chemicals that are used, and the rights of the workers. Begin to calculate the true costs of the food you eat. You may shudder at the thought of eating dogs and cats, but are chickens, turkeys, pigs, cows, and sheep really any different? How intelligent are the animals and aquatic life you eat? Have you ever swum with lobsters, octopuses, turtles, sharks, or fish? Then perhaps you would see how quick and clever they are, how graceful and serene they can be. If you could see them swimming and drifting in their element, then perhaps you would love and respect them more. Perhaps you would get to know their personalities. Perhaps you would see them as more than just a tasty meal.

When you eat a can of tuna, have you considered how they live and die to feed you? Do you wonder if they suffer when they are caught? How many dolphins die alongside them? Do you know the amount of wastewater farm-raised salmon produce and the damage they do to surrounding marine life? Do you know of the antibiotics and pesticides used? Have you stopped to consider how cows and pigs are abused, stunned, and slaughtered? Do you know the reality of factory farming? Do you know of the crowded, cruel conditions of chickens that bring you eggs and breasts and wings? Do you know the life of a dairy cow on a commercial farm? Do you know how the calves are torn from their mothers so their milk can go to humans instead? Do you know these same calves can then be sacrificed to bring you veal and soft-skin leather goods? Yes, it can be sad and tragic to think about, but when God awakens you, you cannot help but be filled with love for all of God's creatures. You will naturally want to consume less, conserve more, and relieve the suffering of all living things.

Only recently have we begun to understand that animals have emotions and fish can experience pain and fear. Only recently have we begun to understand that an infinite Intelligence and a loving Presence moves through all living things. For too long we have known so little, assumed so much, and looked down upon so many. For too long we have engaged in inhumane practices that diminish our collective soul. Perhaps now we need a more spiritual approach to life. Perhaps now we need to educate our children in compassion and cooperation as much as in business, science, and technology. Then future generations might come to know the importance of putting sympathy over efficiency, people over profits, the planet over stockholder interests, animal welfare over wealth, and diplomacy over war. They will see the direct link between caring for humans, loving all sentient beings, protecting our natural resources, and reaping the rewards of peace and prosperity. They will understand the ultimate lesson that we are all connected. They will see clearly that our individual thoughts, words, and actions all add up to create either heaven or hell on Earth.

As we gradually become aware of the unity of all things, we begin to contemplate our collective choices and lifestyles. We ask questions about national and global consumption. Who makes the goods that are bought and sold? How do the companies treat their employees? Where do the profits go? Which of the planet's resources do they use? What is their carbon footprint? Do they do more harm than good? But then we go deeper and ask questions of a more personal nature. We address our individual responsibility and culpability. Do my purchases create a demand for jobs that degrade the lives of others? Do my choices cause other living things to suffer? Does my indifference or inaction contribute to hell on Earth for others? Does my consumption of social media and mass media cause me to see the world askew?

Evolution is the process by which God slowly awakens us to the reality that we are all connected—to him, to the planet, and to each other. He shows us that we are all creatures from the same Creator—whether humans, animals, fish, plants, reptiles, or insects. He opens our eyes to the pain we cause, and he guides us to become more caring and kindhearted. He corrects our follies and shows us how to heal ourselves, heal our relationships, and heal our world.

As humans, we naturally have the greater responsibility of caring for the planet and preserving life. We may not always appear to be the wisest species, but we have learned to control our environment at a more advanced rate than other life forms. If we are not careful, though, our overcontrolling, manipulating, defending, and fighting for territory and resources will be our downfall. That is why we must begin to change and live as one.

Human-induced change throughout history has often been revolutionary and violent. But change can also be evolutionary and peaceful. It can be one person quietly changing her mind, one person changing his behavior for the better, one person working to create a more peaceful home, one person becoming a stable influence, one person embracing a vegan diet, one person using less fossil fuel, and then one by one the world changes. Spirit speaks to us all from within, and one by one we are awakening to a new way of living and relating.

How is God's Spirit speaking to you today? Take some time to think in terms of one. The universe is one. We are all one on planet Earth. What is one thing God is asking of you? Perhaps he is encouraging you to say one kind word to a family member, read one more book to a child, share one more laugh with a friend, walk one more mile in someone else's shoes, plant one more tree, use one less plastic bottle, or go one more day without meat or dairy. One by one is how our world will change. One by one is how together we will bring heaven to Earth.

Until heaven is established, though, planet Earth will be full of challenges and there will be hardships sown into the lining of every life. Sometimes the events of our lives will make no sense at all. Sometimes we will not be able to wrap our minds around the stories we see in the news or the troubles we experience first-hand. From our limited perspective, it will sometimes seem as if there is no God or that he is far removed from our lives. We will ask why God allows bad things to happen and why he seems so insensitive to our plight here on Earth.

The reality, though, is that God is right here with us in the midst of our sorrow and pain. He does not cause our suffering, but he offers a way out. When we reach our breaking point, he holds us together. When we can't go another step, he shows us how. He proves to us our strength, rids us of our illusions, picks us up from the ashes, restores our hope, sets us up for comebacks, and causes us to triumph. He removes us from dark places, dark thoughts, and dark times and puts us in the light. He brings out the goodness and greatness within us. He insists on limits to our suffering, draws us close, and comforts us.

While our problems may seem insurmountable, God knows they are not. So while we may be anxious about the future, he is at peace. He sees every problem that plagues the earth and how each will be resolved. He sees all things from a timeless perspective. He sees where we will be one year from now, one hundred years from now, and even one million years from now. He sees how far we've come and how far we'll go. He sees how things have been and how things will be. He sees us from conception to completion and from here to eternity. He sees the complete arc of our lives and how it shines like a beautiful rainbow.

Nothing can escape God's notice or alter his eternal plans for our lives. He is an island of stability, a center of calm, an upholder of all reality, and a Father who joyously and willingly participates in our lives. Why would you not want to know someone like that?

When we see hardship, God sees a struggle meant to transform us. When we see death, God sees the next exciting stage of our lives. When we are gripped by fear, he moves to release its hold on us. He calms our minds, renews our strength, and leads us gently onward. When we can't see tomorrow, he opens our eyes of faith. When we see difficult days laid out before us, he sees stepping stones of peace, faith, hope, love, and transformation. When we see all manner of obstacles, he sees a curriculum designed to instill resilience, kindness, and joy. He weaves lessons through our days to perfect us. He gives us a depth of character born of experience, reflection, and action.

God has a divine plan to keep us moving onward and upward, to infuse us with love and rid us of all ignorance and insecurity. He has a plan to progressively awaken us as we slowly traverse the universe. When we look up and see an endless, mysterious sky full of dark matter and distant galaxies, God looks around and is at peace in his home. He adorns his abode with quasars, planets, and stars. He populates his living space with material and spiritual beings and makes room for infinitely more. He continuously renovates, adds wings to his home, decorates with love, and transforms his lawn into a play yard for all. Though we may feel like a speck in the universe, a grain of sand in a vast ocean of time and space, it is impossible for us to escape God's watchful care. No matter our place in the cosmos, or the distance from our Father's doorstep, his loving eyes are upon us all, both now and forevermore.

Chapter 7

If you want to live a balanced life, you must decide to make God a part of each day. Spending time with God will help you find the middle way, the way of patience, the way of peace. It will help you avoid extremes in thought, word, and deed. It will help you remember God's goodness and grace. It will help you feel less hurried, as your thoughts will shift from this world to his world, which is eternally calm. It will help you feel less anxious, knowing God is leading you along the right path. It will help you feel more secure, knowing God loves you, even when others may not.

When you spend time with God, you learn you can trust him. You learn you can wait for your true path and purpose to emerge. You learn you can exchange your schedules and timetables for his, which are superior in every way. You learn you can relax, knowing his plans are to prosper you and not to harm you. You learn you can rest because he cares for you. You learn you can be uncannily kind to friends and foes alike, because you have nothing to fear. You learn you can be honest and optimistic because this is God's will. You learn you can actively work to bring heaven to Earth, because he has given you the power and the means to do so.

When you live a balanced life, you can manage the turmoil from within and without, which will continually try to assert itself. You can think clearly, react appropriately, and behave sanely. You can treat others with kindness, dignity, and respect. You can remain calm in the midst of a storm, reliable in the midst of a crisis, and steady in the midst of a struggle. You can walk the path God has prepared for you, and despite any setbacks, you can complete the work he has called you to do.

We are all meant to feel loved, supported, and cared for, but when we are deprived of these conditions, we suffer as individuals and as a society. When we are placed in environments where our basic needs are not met, we can easily fall out of balance. When we find ourselves in situations where we feel helpless, impoverished, or neglected, we can easily become unstable, our immune systems can break down, our mental health erode, and our bodies decline. That is why we must all do our part, however small or consequential, to bring heaven to Earth—to help every person feel loved, seen, protected, and provided for.

When we spend time with God, it does not take long to realize that what we want for ourselves and our families is what we should want for everyone everywhere. Spending time with God naturally makes us more sensitive to others. We become aware of our subtle acts of unkindness. We realize it is no longer enough to live for our own personal gain, with no consideration of how we are affecting others. We become mindful and attuned to what is truly important, and we slowly transition from wanting the good life for ourselves to wanting the good life for all.

When you are in sync with God, you respond more successfully to everyday challenges and interact more comfortably with those around you. You become aware of God's goodness, grace, and guidance flowing through you and your relationships. You give up overreacting to people, overanalyzing past events, and overthinking present-day problems. You become free in spirit. You trust God with the details of your life and accept that he is working all things out for your highest good. You open the windows of your mind and allow fresh air and sunshine to flood the inner rooms. You rid yourself of old, dusty ways of thinking. You develop a brighter outlook on life. You master the art of staying hopeful and helpful in trying times. You set healthy boundaries, express yourself with confidence, and appreciate your unique value in God's eyes. You realize it is acceptable, even essential, to let your light shine and to be an inspiration to others. You remember at all times that God loves you, loves us all, and wants us to be at peace in this world.

Being in sync with God helps us to be more understanding of loved ones and strangers alike. It helps us react good-naturedly to those at home, school, and work. It helps us react graciously and rationally to those on social media. It helps us have compassion for those from faraway places and maybe, one day, from faraway worlds. The universe is teeming with life, and we don't know what tomorrow will bring, but let us begin here and now to develop an appreciation for all living things. If we mistreat ourselves, we open a door for sickness and sorrow to enter. If we mistreat other species, we expose them to pain, stress, disease, the destruction of their habitats, and possible extinction. If we mistreat our planet, we perpetuate the decline of balanced ecosystems and the rise of catastrophic climate change. If we mistreat each other, we invite a descent into hell. But there is always another way, a way back to heaven, a way back to peace and balanced living. It's all up to us.

Living a balanced life prevents a sudden plunge into darkness. It prevents a breakdown in civilized living. It prevents needless suffering. It allows us time to take inventory of our thoughts, words, attitudes, and actions. It helps us pause and reflect on our behavior before we pick a fight, drop a bomb, ignore a problem, overlook a solution, neglect a need, dismiss a human being, or say or do something terribly regrettable. The alternative to balanced living is extreme living, extreme behavior, and extreme consequences. Before you are tempted to veer into the extreme, ask God if a more moderate approach would be helpful.

Certainly there may be occasions when extreme or intense action seems necessary—when you need a dramatic breakthrough or when circumstances are too painful or intolerable to bear. Extreme action can sometimes lead more quickly to freedom, extreme searching more quickly to truth, and extreme effort more quickly to success, but extremes have a flip side, too.

Extreme speech can lead to disgrace, extreme doubt to deadlock, and extreme ambition to disappointment. Extreme power can lead to corruption, and extreme wealth to arrogance and indifference. Extreme suffering can lead to desperation and extreme poverty to crime. Extreme drinking can lead to misery and extreme work to exhaustion. Extreme exercise can lead to collapse and extreme inactivity to illness. Extreme anger can lead to violence, extreme affection to emotional dependency, and extreme introspection to depression. Even extreme religion can lead to fanaticism and extreme faith to recklessness. Therefore, whenever possible, we should try to live peaceful, well-balanced lives.

We should try to express ourselves in ways that unite rather than divide, but sometimes division must precede unity. Sometimes we must resist, separate, and confront authority in order to form a more perfect union. Sometimes chaos and confusion must precede badly needed change. Sometimes individuals, families, institutions, industries, economic systems, and social structures must break down and break apart before heaven can break in. Sometimes before we can realize a lasting peace for all, waters must be muddied and ripples, waves, and even tsunamis sent out. Sometimes everything must dissolve, like a caterpillar within a chrysalis, before something more beautiful can take flight.

When we do finally emerge, we will be the extraordinary creatures God intended us to be. We will be wholly transformed and able to embrace lifestyles of loving-kindness. We will be calmer, gentler, and able to treat others the way we wish to be treated. We will be caring, compassionate, and able to offer warmth and security to all. We will be more hospitable to strangers and more helpful to those who long to belong. We will devote ourselves to making the world a more heavenly home. We will become guardians not only of our own families, but of the entire family of humanity, of all living creatures, and of the planet herself.

God's desire as our Heavenly Parent is for us to learn to get along. He wants us to develop political, social, and economic systems that benefit everyone rather than a few. He wants us to be honest, gracious, and morally upright. He wants us to be purged of all forms of racism, classism, sexism, and speciesism so we may live in peace with all living things. He wants us to be free of all fear, prejudices, and suspicions so we may become a more unified humanity.

You don't need to travel to a faraway country to connect with those who seem different from you. You can engage with people from other cultures, races, and religions all around you. You may just need to walk through your neighborhood, your child's school, the mall, a museum, or an airport. Then open your eyes and remind yourself: God made everyone, he loves us all, and I should learn to love everyone, too. Others may look different, act differently, and think differently, but they are my brothers and sisters, and God wants us to get along. After all, we all bleed alike, we all breathe the same air, we all want what is best for our children, we all want to be loved and accepted, and we all have the same divine destiny. I may see these folks in heaven, so I need to start loving them now, and then I won't have to die to enter heaven, because I will have found it right here on Earth.

God does not want us creating divisions unless separation is needed for our growth, safety, or well-being. He does not ask that we make friends with those who will harm us, but he asks that as we go through life, we try our best to be kind, to make life more bearable for others, to protect the weak, and to provide for those in need. He asks that we do the best we can, whether it is offering our time, resources, or knowledge in service to others. Maybe it's offering someone a ride to the doctor's office, a warm meal, a friendly smile, a listening ear, a piece of advice, a calm response, or a conversation over coffee. Maybe it's something a little larger—dedication to one's family, a teaching career, a scientific discovery, an artistic contribution, a run for office, an honest day's work, or any attempt at improving our world.

Maybe God is simply asking you to show up. Maybe showing up and being present is all that's required for now. Maybe he wants you to be a living witness of his love. Maybe he wants you to be an example of courage and compassion. Maybe he wants you to finish the task he has called you to do despite your fear and trepidation. Maybe he wants you to show composure in the midst of uncertainty or to shed light on a desperate situation. Maybe he needs you to stay in school, stay at home, or stay the course in a long, difficult battle. Maybe he needs you to stand up for what is right despite firm resistance. Maybe he needs you to speak the truth despite widespread doubt and skepticism.

When we learn to govern ourselves individually—through personal displays of kindness, honesty, decency, service, and self-control—we will truly be a great people. When we demonstrate integrity in our personal lives, we will soon demonstrate the same on a broad scale—on a national and international stage. So if you are worried about the future of the planet, the direction your country is taking, or the state of affairs of your government, worry less. Rather, become attuned to the Presence within, and ask yourself each day if you are displaying the fruits, the qualities of God's Spirit, which reside within us all. Allow God to calm you, to combine his mind with your mind, and to blend his personality with yours. Allow him to improve your character and improve your life. Then you will have done your part to improve the world.

As your character improves and your goodness grows, you will begin to see more good in the world than evil, more possibilities than problems, and more sunshine than clouds. You will become a source of light, truth, and hope. You will be drawn to all that is beautiful and true and turn away from all that corrupts and corrodes. You will be like a flower in bloom that has at last found its true purpose. You will make life more pleasant not only for your family but for the entire family of humanity. You will do your part to bring heaven to Earth.

The next time you start to get overwhelmed by anxious thoughts or negative emotions, stop and switch from being an active participant in your problems to an objective observer. Try seeing yourself from above, from a higher perspective. Maybe you are filled with anger or frustration. Maybe you've reached a dead end and are losing all hope. Maybe you are wrestling with a decision or trying to figure out your next step forward. Look down at your struggling self below. Pause and remind yourself that a solution to your troubles is right around the corner. Speak words of encouragement and begin to connect to the Presence within. Remind yourself that help is near, and your pain is temporary. Remind yourself that weeping may last for a night, but joy will come in the morning. Remind yourself that the Creator of the universe loves you and will guide you to a place of perfect peace.

While on Earth, it may seem that we swim through a sea of uncertainty, but God does not abandon us in troubled waters. Our long journey through the open sea is part of his plan to enlighten and perfect us. While we may think we swim alone in a dangerous and shark-infested ocean, God is always with us. He sends dolphins to encircle us and his angels to accompany us. He warms the waters around us. He clears our path of jellyfish. He calms the waves and adjusts the currents. He redirects the shipping lanes and allows us to stay the course. Despite threats all around, he sees us safely to the other side.

While God does not create our sea of hardships, he abides with us through life's marathon swim. He knows that as we swim, we grow in strength and character. With every mile, we become more confident and courageous. When the waves wash over us, we learn devotion to duty. When the shore is out of sight and still a long way off, we learn the importance of faith. When we grow tired and weary, we press on and learn the value of perseverance. In the deepest, darkest waters, we come to know our true fragility and our need for God, family, and friends.

God knows the journey from shore to shore is difficult but transforming. So whatever the consequences, whatever the danger, whatever the struggle, despite the pain, we keep going. We swim to discover our true purpose. We swim because we are dreamers and truth seekers who want more from life. We swim because we are mothers and fathers who want a better way of life for our children. We swim to cast ripples and transform our surroundings. We swim to unite with something larger than ourselves. We swim because God's Spirit propels us forward.

If you find yourself in troubled waters, pause, quiet your mind, and consider your Maker. Even though you might not know what to do, where to go, how to advance, or how to improve your life, God knows. So say a prayer, ask for guidance, and trust God to move you out of your present predicament. Know that when you place your faith in God, you will always be rewarded. But know more still. Know that the measure of your faith will determine your choices, actions, and outcomes in life. Know that the depth of love you have for others will determine the level of love you receive in return. Know that the extent to which you are generous to others will be a predictor of how others will be generous toward you. For whatever you give, and to the degree to which you give it, will always find its way back to you. Therefore, become aware of your thoughts, words, and deeds. Reflect on how you make others feel, for those same feelings will soon well up within you. If you are harsh with others, harshness will find its way to you. If you are gentle and kind, gentleness and kindness will come to you. Maybe not today, but certainly tomorrow, because all that we give away will return to us. How committed are you to your family, friends, work, or a project? Give little, get little. Give much, receive much in return.

You have a tremendous amount of untapped power within you, especially the power to choose. You can choose to trust God. You can choose to believe his promise: that he does not hold any misdeeds against you. If you are weighed down by any burden, ask God to give you a clean conscience, a pure heart, a free spirit, and a renewed joy. Then allow him to transform you from the inside out. Choose today to combine your will with his will. Choose to allow a bright future to unfold. Choose to work with the Presence within so you may develop a new way of thinking, behaving, and reacting to life.

When someone pushes your buttons or circumstances upset you, choose patience, restraint, and self-control. Choose to have a sense of humor, to forgive, and to overlook small offenses. Choose not to become defensive, take the bait, raise the temperature, or take things too personally. Choose to walk away and tell yourself it's not that important, not worth losing your peace or damaging a relationship. Choose to return good for evil. Choose to believe a perfect solution for your problem will appear.

Whenever you are in the middle of a difficult situation, remember God is on your side. He sees every temptation that comes against you and every problem that confronts you. He knows when you are under pressure and when your thoughts are racing out of control. He sees everything going on in your life. He knows when you are at the top of your game and when you have grown quietly desperate. He knows what you will face long before you face it, and he knows how to deliver you from every difficulty.

God's love for us does not fluctuate according to our actions, thoughts, or attitudes. His love is constant and unconditional. We can act up, lash out, shut down, give up, drop out, disappoint, and do all manner of thoughtless, unkind things, but nothing can move God to love us less. Even if we live perfect lives and are blessed beyond our wildest dreams, he cannot love us more than he already does. His love is complete, everlasting, and unchanging. There is nothing in the entire universe, seen or unseen, that can separate us from his love. We may move away from God, but his love for us is eternally fixed.

We may have little time for God, but our Heavenly Parent has all the time in the world for us. Time is his device to draw us together as one. Like a father sitting on the doorstep of his home, God sees you far off and looks forward to your homecoming. Perhaps you have been away too long. Perhaps you have been busy getting by in the world. Perhaps you are still too far off to see that he is coming for you. Perhaps you do not recognize the one who rushes to meet you. How quickly your day will change when at last you fall into your Father's arms. How warm his embrace will be when at last you find the rest you need. Even now he rushes to welcome you, if only you will receive him. Even now he waits to hear all that troubles you. Even now he wishes to remind you that your sins are forgiven and remembered no more.

When we experience difficulties and hardships in life, hear of troubling events around the world, or read of dire predictions for the planet, it may be easy to think God has abandoned us or perhaps does not exist. But nothing could be further from the truth. God is not far off in Paradise, unaware of our problems and all that plagues the earth. He is here, comforting us, helping us unite our world, heal our planet, and discover his Presence within. "Does he who made the ear, not hear? Does he who formed the eye, not see?"

Problems may overtake us, we may lose our way, but when we begin to connect to the Divine within, we will have every reason to hope again and every reason to smile. When we connect with God, our sanity is restored, our confusion dissolved, our temptations removed, and our way made clear. A vision of how to move forward is brought to mind, and we are inspired to take right action. Solutions to our problems appear, and peace returns to us.

God's plans may seem perplexing and our progress slow, but we can be sure of this: God is good, we can trust him, and contrary to what we may think, he is actively involved in the affairs of our lives. He is endlessly working to elevate us to higher states of love, joy, freedom, understanding, and goodness. So before you allow yourself to be defeated by the circumstances of life, realize God lives within you, within all of us, and is working everything out for our highest good.

You were not born into this world feeling dispirited and dejected. You arrived with a powerful life force flowing through your veins. You arrived full of promise, a unique creation, and beloved by God. So if you are feeling lost or overcome, remember there was a time when you were confident, carefree, and brimming with energy and possibility. No one is born with negative thoughts and attitudes. No baby ever comes out thinking they should give up, throw in the blanket, and call it quits. Life, though, has a way of wearing us down. People disappoint us, circumstances change, responsibilities mount, dreams are dashed, problems overwhelm us, doubts overtake us, our bodies fail us, and before long we're feeling like the walking dead. But we are not meant to live this way.

Starting today you can rid yourself of all that drains your joy and be filled with a powerful sense of purpose. The power to change is within you. Are you ready to call on your Creator for help? Are you ready to exchange bad days for better ones? Are you ready to prune yourself of harmful habits? Are you ready to surrender limiting beliefs and focus on new possibilities? Are you ready to feel at peace with yourself and the world?

If you feel stuck in any area of your life, reach out to God today. Let him help you break free of the quagmire of negative thinking that has you feeling trapped. Ask God to throw you a lifeline, and then be prepared to work with him to free yourself. It may take some time, it may take some effort, but trust God through the process. Commit yourself to improved daily routines that will help revitalize you, propel you forward, and turn your life into a beautiful adventure.

Despite painful circumstances, disappointments, or any lack of love you may be feeling, know there is One who watches over you who loves you more tenderly than a mother, who guards you more carefully than a father, and who walks closer to you than the dearest friend. Take a moment to ask God to renew your mind and cleanse your thoughts of all that brings you low. Tell him you are ready to soar with the eagles and be free.

Maybe you lack a sense of purpose, and try as you may, you can't hear God's voice, feel his presence, or understand what you should be doing. We are not always conscious of the ways God is working in our lives, but he is, so be patient. It takes time to figure life out. It takes prayer, study, meditation, and contemplation to discern the will of God. Maybe God is not asking you to do anything but rather to become someone. Maybe he is leading you to be more hopeful and helpful, more focused and forgiving, more genuine and caring, and more fully prepared for the larger work he will soon call you to do.

Perhaps you think you're too old to make a difference. Perhaps you are bedridden and feel your best years are behind you. You can still pray. You can still listen. You can still make a phone call, connect to others, write a letter, or offer an encouraging word. You can still light up someone's day just with your presence. You can offer a young person a sense of comfort and security. You can share a story. You can recall a memory. You can make something with your hands and cheer someone up. Don't doubt your ability to bring sunshine into someone's life. You can be an example to someone of how to age gracefully, how to live responsibly, how to be a devoted grandparent, a good neighbor, a good person. You don't know who may be watching you. If you're alive, you have a lot to offer whether you know it or not.

Maybe you have the opposite problem—you think you're too young to make a difference. How can that be? You have youth and time on your side. You have energy and vitality at your disposal. You have your whole life ahead of you. You have dreams to pursue, thoughts to share, places to visit, music to make, books to read, people to love, children to raise, and maybe even aliens to meet. Who knows, you may be the first generation on Earth to meet travelers from a distant planet. You have a bright future ahead of you that is slowly unfolding. Be patient. Don't worry that you can't see your future from A to Z. If God wanted you to know every detail about your life, he would show you. He is trying to develop your faith. He is hoping to surprise you. Trust that God is leading you to become a person of great strength, courage, kindness, influence, talent, beauty, and goodness. God is using you to change the world and bring heaven to Earth. He is also preparing you for eternity, so stay connected to him each day. Allow him to lead you to be a good friend, a good son or daughter, a good person. You will soon be grown, so for now, learn to appreciate each day, and allow God to lead you through the exciting journey of youth.

We are here only for a short while to experience life on Earth and to learn lessons unique to our human condition, and then we go on to another realm, to another way of life, to another body. So while we are here, we should make the most of our lives. We should ask questions and seek answers. We should commit ourselves to our families. We should work to help others. We should strive to know God, who, though invisible, has a true personality. Indeed, he is the original personality within our universe, and he desires to be known.

God is loving and ever so kind. He patiently watches over us, waiting as we awaken to all that he is. He sends messengers to guide us and his Spirit to indwell us. He shields us from eternal harm, provides for our loving care, and when we depart this Earth, he continues to uphold us. He lays out a divine plan for each of us and carries us from age to age through eternity. Do you think your life will end in the grave? Think again, and consider the kindness of your Creator. His plans for you are not limited to a few short years on Earth. God's plan for you is an endless revelation of beauty, truth, fellowship, and love.

God lives both in and out of time and in and out of space. He is not confined by anything. He sets the boundaries of creation and knows the farthest realms of the universe. He knows the number of all planets and stars. He knows the names of all living things. He knows your thoughts, fears, and delights. He knows the moment of your conception, all stages of your life, and your journey beyond this world. But why wait for another body and another realm of life to acknowledge God? Why keep him at a distance? He waits so patiently as you pass by, but do not mistake this patience for indifference. Though he appears to be in no hurry, as evolution is long and eternity is beyond our comprehension, he earnestly waits. He longs for you to sit and stay awhile. He longs to talk with you, but he will not compel you to take his hand. But why put off his kindness? Why wait for peace with your Creator when it is available here and now?

Time is God's invention to move us closer to him in phases, to unify our world, to make us aware of all that is and all that we can become. Time drawn out can only offer you the same result—oneness with God, peace, joy, freedom, and unconditional love. It all waits for you within yourself and within the bubble of time and space. It is life's grand adventure to explore this world God has made, but to move through life without God is to suffer. Why suffer when you can take the hand of One who loves you, who can lead you out of all struggle and heartache, and who can unite you with your brothers and sisters on Earth? Why cling to old ways of thinking and old ways of seeing the world when

God is offering you a fresh new outlook? Why stay trapped and bound when you can be free?

With God's help you can choose new thoughts, new relationships, and a new way of living. You can be released from a painful past and move joyfully into tomorrow, which holds so much promise. God would give you a fresh new perspective on life, if only you would take one small step of faith to bridge the gap between a sad reality without him and a peaceful existence with him. God is gladly offering you a life of purpose and eternal security. So decide today to turn to him. Decide to shut out all that would disturb your peace. Sit quietly, even if for one small moment, and venture to connect to the Presence within. Decide to accept the goodness of God. Decide to see the good within yourself. Decide to see the good within everyone. For just a moment, imagine you are one with God and one with all humanity.

Chapter 8

It's good to get advice from other people when making decisions, to study a matter thoroughly, to figure out the pros and cons, and to weigh everything in the balance, but don't forget God's input. God, more than anyone, knows the best path forward for your life. He knows your personality, your strengths and weaknesses, your potential, and the environment where you will grow and thrive. He knows what will bring you joy and contentment. He knows the temptations, obstacles, and pitfalls that will confront you, and he can lead you through and around them all. He knows how to help you discover your true calling and find the right people and opportunities to enhance your life. He knows how to help you bring heaven to mind, heaven into your home, and heaven to Earth.

In order for God to guide you, you must first be willing to accept that he is your highest, wisest confidant. Then you must be willing to listen and trust him. Making choices based on divine guidance will have lasting rewards, but it will not always lead to an easy path forward. With guidance must also come a commitment to grow, to change, to move beyond your comfort zones, and to stretch your faith. It will require courage, dedication, and patience to become the person God is calling you to be. It will require staying the course and completing the work he is asking you to do.

We live in a culture where the development of one's character is not always highly valued. The virtues of peace, patience, kindness, goodness, faithfulness, gentleness, and self-control are often overlooked. Instead, we see too frequently that might is right, loud is strong, and meek is weak. We see that profits are prized over basic human rights, wealth is worshiped, instant gratification is encouraged, and rabbits are favored over tortoises. Rabbits hurry through life, but they don't always cross the finish line first. Sometimes slow and steady wins the race. When we slow down, we can make better decisions. We can avoid mistakes. We can get in touch with God's Spirit and decide if our actions serve a higher purpose.

Don't think you need to be a jackrabbit to reach your goals. When you move at a slower pace, you have more time to think, reflect, and sense how God is guiding you. You avoid making rash decisions with harmful consequences. Yes, it may take longer than you would like to reach your goals, but if you move honestly and persistently in the direction of your calling, you will one day reap amazing rewards. You may or may not end up rich financially, but you will end up rich in character, rich in personal satisfaction, rich in reputation, rich in faith, rich in inner peace, rich in raising children who can weather the storms of life, and richer still in the world to come.

As a tortoise, you may not be able to run the fastest along the path, but you will be able to avoid obstacles that would trip you up. You will be guided around snares that would entangle you, harm you, or delay your progress. You will gain the momentum and confidence needed to keep moving forward. Without rushing through life, you will be more in touch with God's goodness and grace. Rabbits love the limelight, but as a tortoise your life can be pleasant, and you can reach your goals quietly and successfully without falling into temptation. You can steadily move in the direction God is leading you while having a positive, lasting influence on those along your path.

But maybe you're not a rabbit or a tortoise. Maybe you're more like a sloth. Sloths have a bad reputation, because they can be even slower than tortoises, but we can learn a lot from sloths. Slowing down to the pace of a sloth might sometimes be helpful. It might give you an excuse to rest. It might keep you from leaping before you look or speaking before you think. It might keep you from overworking or overspending. It might keep you from tackling life's problems in your own way and in your own strength. Oftentimes we think we need to do more to fix our problems when we might need to do less. Slowing down to the pace of a sloth may be good for a season. It may give you time to heal. It may lead you to new thoughts and insights. It may lead you to a new way of relating to others. It may lead to new people who will lead you in a positive new direction. Sometimes it's okay to act like a sloth; to sit quietly and move slowly. Before you are slowed down involuntarily by life, try slowing down on your own and connecting with God.

We are all here to advance and to awaken to the Presence within. We are all here to become Godlike in character, to love one another, and to make the world a better place, but none of this can happen overnight. So be patient. Slow down. Allow God to strengthen you and prepare you for a higher calling. Allow him to restore your sense of peace and possibility. If you do this, it will create a ripple effect that will spread from within you to your home, to your community, to your country, and even to the whole world. Countries don't rise and fall because of the economic and political decisions of their leaders. The rise and fall of nations is due to the collective, daily decisions of their citizens. So choose today to make wise decisions. Choose to make life bearable for those around you. Choose not to be indifferent to the pain and suffering of others. Choose to promote peace, health, opportunity, and freedom for all.

Perhaps all that is required of you today is the little effort you can give to improving yourself, which in turn will help improve our world. Perhaps all you can offer is a prayer, a quiet reflection, a moment of meditation, a more hopeful thought, or a dream of a better tomorrow. Even God was quiet before bringing the universe into existence. It takes time to plan, to think, to imagine, and to visualize how you would like your life to unfold. It's okay to be quiet and take your time; that's part of the creative process.

Praying, reading, thinking, listening, reworking ideas, reframing pictures in your mind, deciding on the right course of action, imagining the possibility of something new, all require quiet effort. Eventually you will be ready, and you will know the direction to take.

As creative beings, we are always fighting against our actual selves in favor of our potential selves. We want bigger, better, more beautiful lives. We want results now and not tomorrow, so when things don't go our way, or when we don't get what we want when we want it, we can easily grow frustrated, stir up discontent, and sometimes make everyone around us miserable. If only we could just settle down, behave ourselves, and accept our circumstances in a dignified manner. But we can't.

God has given us a dual nature. We are both evolutionary beings and spiritual beings. He has filled us with certain animal instincts and desires, which have allowed our species to survive over millions of years, yet he has also placed his Spirit within us and called us to a higher way of living. Within each one of us are selfish, grasping, sensual desires and cravings, which exist alongside our higher longings for love, joy, beauty, peace, truth, and freedom. It is entirely natural to want more from life, but God has put us on a path toward perfection, so our ongoing challenge is to tame our lower nature in favor of a higher one.

Learning to regulate our emotions demonstrates self-control, and getting along peacefully with others helps us make evolutionary leaps in living. We have arrived at a point in time where worldwide cooperation is now essential for our survival. Prior to the last century, all that really mattered was learning to get along with family, friends, and neighbors. Selfish behavior, poor choices, and wrong attitudes could quickly put you on the path to becoming a social outcast, but it couldn't do any worldwide harm. You had to learn to get along at a local level, or it could affect your livelihood, your standing in the community, or the welfare of your family, or even cost you your life. In some cases, you had the option of fleeing to another town or country and starting over again. People still do that today, but now when you flee, your criminal record, credit scores, and social status follow you. Your reputation precedes you, and the internet is always there to remind you of your past. We can run, but we can't hide.

The world may be our oyster, as Shakespeare once said, with pearls of opportunity, but today our oyster is filled with grids, greenhouse gases, free-floating viruses, weapons of mass destruction, space satellites, government surveillance systems, the internet, social media, crowded cities, transcontinental flights, and international commerce. Today within the oyster, there is an ever-present connectedness and an endless flow of people, resources, microbes, and information. Now our neighbors are those in neighboring countries. Now if our leaders show irresponsible behavior, we can suffer devastating consequences. Now if we don't cooperate with one another, the environment can deteriorate, wars can break out, diseases can spread, economies can collapse, and social unrest can ensue.

Before we can learn to live together on a global level, we must learn to cooperate on a local level, and before we can successfully cooperate on a local level, we must learn to cooperate within our families, and before harmony can come to our families, we must find peace within. God is first and foremost interested in you as an individual. He is not so much concerned with saving the world as he is with saving you. He desires to be in a relationship with you in a way that is personal and pleasant. He wants to open your eyes and show you a new way of living. He wants you to slow down long enough to hear the heartstrings within. He wants you to tune in to your inner music. He wants you to know that when you take time to connect with the Divine, all manner of blessings will result.

We cannot go about changing the world until we have had a transformation on the inside. Maybe you're frustrated by a relationship, your finances, the environment, the government, the pandemic, or any number of important social issues. You've spend a great deal of time worrying, complaining, and complying. But now you've grown increasingly frustrated and angry. There is no shame in showing anger. Controlled anger can actually be very constructive. It's just when we blow up again and again that things can go wrong. Have you ever boiled eggs? The ideal way to boil eggs is to put them in cold water, bring them to a slow boil, and then remove the pot from the source of heat. If you let them boil too long, they might crack because the water is churning too violently. But if you let the eggs rest in the hot water once they've reached the boiling point, you'll have perfectly cooked hard-boiled eggs.

In the same way, there is nothing wrong about being angry. It's a part of life, it's a natural emotion, and there are a lot of people and situations that can make us angry. Prolonged anger, however, can hurt us. There is nothing wrong with letting off steam, but blowing your top and spewing hot lava everywhere can cause lasting damage. It can change the landscape around you. It can destroy homes, cause people to flee, and leave you with a costly cleanup. So before you wreak havoc on your relationships, damage your health, or do something you might regret, decide to channel your anger into something productive and positive. Maybe you'll be motivated to change a bad habit, change your opinion of someone to see them in a new and softer light, or change your routine to find peace within and help bring heaven to your patch of earth.

In dealing with life's problems, we don't have to run around frenzied and frustrated or dwell endlessly on all that's troubling us. Sometimes we just need to sit quietly and seek wise counsel within ourselves. When we are overwhelmed by life, when we are angry or frustrated, when we are worrying excessively, or when we are turning too often to technology for relief, we are sacrificing opportunities to pray, ponder, listen, and connect to the Divine within. Sometimes we just need to be still, like an egg sitting quietly in a pot of water. Because in our stillness, we allow the creative process room to operate. In our stillness, we allow God time to perfect us.

Begin today to look within. What does God want you to accomplish? Who does he desire you to be on the inside? What sort of life does he want you to live? We each have unique personalities, gifts, and talents, and if we stay close to God, he can help us take advantage of all these to reach our highest potential. Remember, our time on Earth is short, so we should each do the best we can with what we've been given. When we pursue agendas not in alignment with God's will, we are unfortunately wasting time, resources, and energy. Why would you want to spend your whole life or even a small part of it pursuing goals that go against God's best plan for your life? For your family? For humanity? For the planet? Your plans may seem to pay off in the short run, but in the long run, the labor you put into pursuing your own agenda will be in vain.

When they built the Titanic, they thought it was unsinkable. It was the largest, most luxurious cruise ship ever built. It took over four years of planning and construction to complete, and it required the work of more than 15,000 men. It was as long as two and a half football fields and had the capacity to carry over 3,500 passengers. It had all the most modern conveniences—cafes, lounges, Turkish baths, a gymnasium, a swimming pool, libraries, a grand staircase, and beautifully decorated rooms. But on April 12, 1912, on its very first voyage out of the dock, it hit an iceberg. Less than three hours later, the ship they thought was unsinkable was two miles below on the ocean floor, and over 1,500 passengers had perished. What happened?

Experts say part of the problem was hasty construction, poorly designed iron rivets that held the ship together, and an unnecessary rush to cross the Atlantic in record time. But the most serious problem of all was the failure of critical decision makers to listen. Every step of the way, if they had slowed down, listened to the voice within, and listened to the concerns and warnings of others, the outcome could have been different. The Titanic could have been a marvel of engineering and workmanship. The workers could have been proud of their work. Families could have joyously received their loved ones upon their arrival in New York. It could have had a long history and been enjoyed by thousands of passengers for decades. The Titanic could have even served as a hospital ship during World War I and helped relieve the suffering of thousands. But everyone who played a part in the planning, financing, design, construction, and navigation of the boat had to do their best in order for the Titanic to have been a lasting success.

The same is true in our lives today. If we fail to do our best, cut corners, become complacent, ignore warning signs, put our egos first, and become overly concerned about our reputations or the bottom line, we too can play a role in a sinking ship. What ship are you a part of today? Is it your family? Your business? Your community? Your country? Your planet? Are you making wise decisions? Are you speaking up when you need to? Are you listening to those who need to be heard? Are you being kind and respectful to those around you? Are you thinking of the needs of others as much as your own? Are you acting as though you are part of a global family? Slow down and ask God every day to help you make the best possible choices. You might still make mistakes, but they will be minor compared to the chaos that can result when you don't involve God or attempt to understand what he wants for you and for everyone.

God's standards of success and the world's standards are often diametrically opposed, so if you're not careful, you might think you're living the good life, when in fact you're sailing on the Titanic. On the Titanic everything was glamourous and new. Everyone felt so fortunate to be aboard. Certainly they must have thought God's favor had fallen on them until tragedy struck.

It is easy to be misled into thinking prosperity and material abundance equate to God's favor. All that society values—wealth, good health, good fortune, and a good name—are not the result of God's favoritism, but of choices we make, choices made by those who came before us, and choices we make collectively within the family of humanity. Just as God does not cast favor upon some, neither does he cast judgment upon others, as there is no mean-spiritedness within him. God's generosity and unconditional love fall evenly upon all, upon rich and poor alike.

We are all on an invisible spiritual path, and we are all being pruned and prepared for greater things to come. Often those who appear the least successful among us are in fact racing down a spiritual highway and advancing in spiritual maturity. Therefore, we should never envy what others have or judge others by what they don't have, because those you look down upon may in fact be entering the kingdom of God ahead of you. For as Jesus said, "Many who are first shall be last, while the last shall often be first."

God is always moving us in the direction of perfection, and he knows when we are ready to advance, when we need to repeat a lesson, or when we just need to rest. If we take our eyes off of God, we can easily begin comparing ourselves to others. We can lose sight of what God wants for us and set sail on a Titanic of our own making. It's fine to want more from life, but don't be so easily frustrated by all you don't have. Place your hope in God that he will continue to lead you upward, enlarge your life, enlighten your mind, help you see the good in others, and surround you with opportunities for service and growth. Ask God for guidance and direction for your life. Let him give you a new way of living that will allow you to be calmer, more confident, and a blessing to others.

Throughout the day, give yourself permission to slow down, turn inward, and listen to the quiet voice within. What is the Creative Spirit saying? What is God calling you to do? Are your dreams in alignment with his will for your life? Do those around you cause you to desire more of what they want and less of what God wants? The passengers on the Titanic enjoyed great opulence. They dined so well and ate from gold-plated dishes. They danced and laughed and marveled at their good fortune. Yet it all ended in tragedy. But for you, if you're headed in the wrong direction, there is still time to turn the ship around. There is still time never to board the ship at all.

When your life finally ends here on Earth, you cannot carry your material wealth forward, but you can carry forward your wealth of character, your lessons learned, your perfected personality, and your personal accomplishments. The record will show the way you overcame obstacles, the way you raised your children, how you made others feel, and how you made the world around you a better place. This will be credited to you in the life to come.

When you are gone from Earth, you may or may not leave a monetary inheritance, but you can leave your friends and loved ones with memories to cherish. Perhaps you will be remembered fondly as a loving relative, a faithful friend, a kind neighbor, a patient teacher, a strong leader, a stable presence, or a beautiful soul who uplifted others. You might be remembered for promoting peace, spreading joy, furthering justice, beautifying the world, helping the poor, or healing the planet. You may be remembered for your service and sacrifice, your devotion and care, or your courage and commitment. You might be remembered for your quiet humility, your bold outspokenness, or something in between.

Decide today how you would like to be remembered, form an ideal in your mind, and then resolve to close the gap between where you are now and where you would like to be in the future. But don't try to advance in your own strength and in your own way. Lean on God each day so that you can become the person you were born to be. Decide to work in harmony with God, and then see your life naturally unfold, like a flower opening to the sun.

God understands how difficult life can sometimes be. He understands how easily we can give up—on hope, on love, on people, on dreams of a bright tomorrow. He understands our vulnerabilities, all the ways evolution has handicapped us and all the strikes against us. But in the midst of it all—the personal disappointments, political dysfunction, economic inequality, racial disparity, religious confusion, and climate catastrophes—God speaks to us. He invites us in, out of the raging storms of life, and has us leave our troubles at the door.

God is not human; he is a loving Heavenly Father, so he is never indifferent to what we are facing. He is not pretending our problems will go away on their own. He is actively involved with us, inviting us daily to partner with him. But the decision to partner with God is ours; he has given us free will to act alone or to live in harmony with him. One person acting alone can live a life for better or for worse, but one person united with God can only live a better life. One person going within can find peace and purpose. One person guided by God's Spirit can help others overcome the difficulties and disappointments of life.

God has placed a key deep within each one of us that has the power to change our lives and to change the world. It is only when we sincerely seek him, though, that this key will turn and we will connect to the Spirit of Truth. As we each do our part to connect with God, he does his part to join our hearts and minds, until at last our world becomes a happier place and a more beautiful home.

Let us have faith in God's divine plan. Where we stand divided, let us look for common ground. Let us create a culture of kindness that radiates out from within each one of us. If you've had an adversarial relationship with someone, begin now to change your way of thinking and relating. Try a nicer thought, a different tone of voice, a less offensive word, a more relaxed posture, or a softer approach. Try listening, forgiving, and smiling. Try taking things less personally. Try having a more hopeful attitude and a more positive outlook.

Change may not come in a day, but it will come eventually if you make a sincere effort. Plant a seed, and then keep watering and weeding. Keep persisting in your efforts and look for signs of growth. Recognize the role you play in every relationship. Are you contentious and short-tempered? Do you like to debate every subject and regularly win? Do you criticize more than you compliment? Do you always get your way at the expense of peace? Do you anticipate negative comments and reactions from others? What if you started to change your ways? What if you began to see the good in others? Because within everyone, there is actual goodness. It may seem like a tiny grain of goodness in some, but don't give up. God created us to live in harmony with each other, but he knows you can't do it in your own strength. So ask him to soften your heart and open your eyes. Ask him to help you get through the tough conversations, the impossible relationships, and the stressful situations. Ask him to help you overcome your biases and prejudices and see everyone on Earth as part of your extended family.

Making the change from being a fault finder to a peacemaker is not easy. But just as you may have formed a habit of being critical, argumentative, or easily offended, you can form a new habit of being peaceful, kinder, and more understanding. You can train your mind in the art of gracious behavior. God is in the business of building and sustaining relationships, and his divine plan includes bringing people together, forming friendships, supporting families, building communities, and helping people grow and learn from one another. Relationships are one of the most important tools God offers to awaken us; they are the key to our success, growth, and self-discovery.

God wants for us what all good parents want for their children—for us to learn to get along. No parents like to see their children fighting and arguing, but they know sometimes it's a necessary part of growing up. Likewise, God doesn't mind a little wrestling and complaining, but he would like to hear some laughter too. In addition to all the shouting, he would like to hear some singing. At the end of the day, he would like to see us living in harmony, but how do any of us learn to play well with others, to be respectful and kind? Usually the hard way. We go through years of growing pains and stubborn ways. Why compromise when you can bully your way through a bad situation? Why lose face when you can distort the truth? Some have become experts at bullying, blaming, complaining, and lying. We do this to shut down our critics, win arguments, get our way, and protect our egos, but this behavior will only get us so far. At some point we will hit a brick wall and be forced to change. Why? Because God's goodness lives within each one of us, and eventually it will be drawn out.

God is not fond of chaos, but he will allow it. He is not fond of callousness and cruelty, but he will allow it. God is not fond of boastful, narcissistic behavior, but he will allow it. He is not fond of selfishness and dishonesty, but he will allow it. Up to a point. At some point he will draw the line and put an end to bad behavior. At some point he will move to humble us, and in doing so he will have moved us one step closer to perfection.

We have all been given a free will to act as we please, but we've also been born into a universe with divine laws and consequences woven into the fabric of our existence. We can only get away with bad behavior for so long, and then it will catch up to us. God's will for us is to walk in humility and to love one another. So if you have taken on an aggressive, self-centered, divisive, or overly competitive approach to life, God will not allow it to continue forever. At some point you will be shown a better way. At some point you will learn that patience does not equal powerlessness and kindness is not a personal failure. Perhaps your behavior has paid off handsomely in the short run, but it is the long run that matters most to God. He is interested in preparing you for eternity. He is interested in moving you in the direction of perfection.

Kindness is the way of God, the way of perfection, and calmness is the result of a peaceful approach to life. It is the natural consequence of seeking to imitate God, just as freedom is the natural reward for choosing to do God's will. And what is God's will? Look to Gandhi, Mother Teresa, or Martin Luther King Jr., or maybe just look to your grandmother. What do they have in common? Did they promote hatred, violence, and bigotry? No, they were peacemakers. And they helped pave the way for heaven on Earth.

Jesus said, "Seek first the kingdom of heaven," because he understood that heaven contains the ideal conditions where peace, love, and perfect community abide. One of the highest callings we have is to learn to live in harmony with others; to learn to love one another despite our many differences. It is a high calling and a difficult one. We cannot do it in our own strength, so we must develop a habit of depending on God for help. In doing so, we will be taught the art of overlooking small offenses, responding calmly, having faith in positive outcomes, working to resolve problems collectively, and building peaceful communities.

Pursuing a peaceful agenda, though, does not mean we should be indifferent to evil or ignorant of the law, but as much as we are able, we should be slow to anger, quick to forgive, and always willing to make a positive difference in the lives of others. Each day we should look for ways to relate to our neighbors in a healthy manner, to mend fences when necessary, to scowl less and smile more.

If you are in an environment where you're having difficulty with someone, and you can't seem to escape them, you should ask yourself if there is something to be learned from this experience. Rather than fighting against the situation or avoiding the person, pause and ask God if anything good can come from this. What would God have you learn? What would God have you do or say? Perhaps if you understood the lesson, the problem as you see it would disappear. Many problems we have in life revolve around our inability or unwillingness to love, listen, speak up, express our feelings, set healthy boundaries, and forgive.

If you're struggling with unforgiveness, you don't have to maintain a relationship with the one who's hurt you in order to forgive. Working up to a point of forgiveness can take time, sometimes years, but eventually it is possible to reach a bold decision to let go of your past. A deeper understanding of yourself will emerge, followed by a desire to surrender your pain and free your mind. Sometimes no words will be necessary between you and the one you're forgiving; no face-to-face conversation needed. God will then either restore your relationship at some point or help you end it and move on. He doesn't want you walking around with the weight of the world on your shoulders, so begin to let go of any troubling thoughts that are wearing you down and keeping you from moving forward. Let him give you the strength and courage needed to release a painful past. Begin to accept that you were made to live in a state of dignity, grace, freedom, and peace. God wants that for you and for all of his children. So, starting today, allow him to guide you through any difficulty you may be facing. Let him help you soften your heart, free your mind, take your focus off of a painful past, forgive yourself and others, and imagine a brighter tomorrow.

God can also help us overcome our prejudices and cultural biases. Because wherever we go in life, we will always find people who are different from ourselves. They may come from different countries, have different personalities, speak differently, eat different foods, and have different customs, but they are still part of our extended family. As God's children, they all have a spark of the Divine within. Therefore, we should do our best to get along, to consider everyone's needs, and to respect everyone's dreams as much as our own. We should try to extend a little more kindness to all living beings, because as God looks out on our world and on all worlds throughout the universe, he has one simple message: Love one another, as I love you.

Chapter 9

When we think of heaven, we might think of being surrounded by unconditional love; waking up to the presence of angels, Jesus, or God; uniting with family and friends; or suddenly arriving in a fairy-tale-like setting with forests, waterfalls, rainbows, and unparalleled beauty. Often we're too busy in this life to think about the afterlife, but if we were to imagine that all the above is true, the next question might be: Then what?

We will certainly be overwhelmed by heaven's brilliance, but if life is eternal, our stay there will be for a very long time; so long that it is beyond our ability to comprehend. In one lifetime on Earth, we may live one hundred years, so we are incapable of fathoming the concept of eternity. We know intuitively, though, that there must be something beyond this life. No one likes to imagine a future involving their complete obliteration, a complete absence of existence. Most people, if they're honest, even honest atheists, hope they're headed somewhere wonderful after death, a place far better than this planet with all of its toil and turmoil. A place where there is no disease, debt, depression, disasters, or death. We won't have bills to pay, dishes to wash, doctors to visit, or bodies to mend. We won't have wars, pandemics, politics, and ecological disasters to worry about. We won't have ugly thoughts and attitudes to contend with. We won't have deadlines and dead-end jobs. We'd like to think we'll be transported to a place that is beautiful and sunny and where we'll always be happy.

Hanging out with everyone and relaxing in beautiful surroundings for eternity might get old after a while, though. Imagine being on an extended vacation. Despite the refreshing change of scenery, you might eventually grow restless. The initial feeling of exhilaration might gradually diminish, until one day you wake up feeling a little less excited and start looking around for something new to do. When we arrive in heaven, it must be heavenly, so by definition there must be an absence of not only suffering, strife, disease, and poverty, but also boredom. To be heavenly, it must offer a perfect balance of love, joy, beauty, provision, and peace.

With eternity being so long and drawn out, perhaps what we call heaven is not a single destination but an unfolding: an endless series of lifetimes, destinations or experiences that spiritualize us and move us closer to God. Perhaps we should not think of our transition from Earth as a one-time occasion that lands us in the heart of Paradise. Maybe we're not quite ready to be in the full presence of God. Going from here to there, with no stops in between, might be too shocking and disorienting. It would be like a child falling asleep in his crib and waking up at the top of Mount Everest. The child would be completely confused and unable to understand where he was. Mount Everest might be a wonderful destination for a lot of people. Many would appreciate the view, but suddenly transporting a child to the top of the world would be overwhelming and senseless. It would serve no purpose, and there would be nothing for him to appreciate.

On the other hand, if the child spent his life preparing to ascend Mount Everest, it would be an entirely different experience. What if he were raised hearing stories about the mountain and seeing pictures and films about various climbers and expeditions? What if he were educated in mountaineering from his youth, and gradually developed a keen sense of respect and appreciation for the mountain? What if he trained and conditioned while preparing for his eventual ascent? What if he made friends with other climbers and Sherpas, who gave him a true sense of what to expect? And then, after years of hard work, what if he set out and made it successfully to the top? Then he would have a real sense of accomplishment and an understanding of what it means to ascend the tallest mountain on Earth. Then he would realize the value of his long journey and the necessity of every stage of preparation. Then he would look around in awe and have a full appreciation of the view from the top.

God wants to be known, to close the gap between us, but there is a vast difference between creature and Creator. Therefore, he must gradually awaken us to all that he is and all that we can become. Everything he does is thoughtful, intentional, and motivated by loving-kindness. Just as he is trying to make us good citizens of this world, God wants us to one day become good heavenly citizens. But we are still in our early childhood years, and God does not wish to tear us away from all that is familiar. He is not in the business of shocking and scaring his children.

He's in the business of perfecting us, nurturing us, educating us, and helping us gently transition from one stage of life to the next.

The universe is wide, and we cannot know all the good God has planned for us. We cannot know the specifics of what life will be like on the other side or where we will be going once we depart these bodies. We can wonder about our next life, but we can never form a completely clear picture.

Imagine life as a game of soccer or football, and you are confined to a stadium where the game is being played. Further imagine that you've never been outside this stadium. People enter, but you don't know where they've come from, and people exit, but you don't know where they're going. You just know you're at the game with lots of people for a certain amount of time, and when it's over, you will all leave. While you're there, you don't think too much about what will happen after the game, because the game itself is so full of action and excitement. You cheer, you curse, you're up, you're down; you fully participate. Maybe you're a spectator or a player, a coach, a referee, a concessions worker, or a linesman. No matter. What's important is that you're at the game, and life in the stadium is the only life you know. Well, that's our limited view of life on Earth from our human perspective.

Now imagine God's perspective. Step back a few trillion light years. He has a broader view. He sees the stadium as well as life beyond the stadium walls. He has a view to which you are not yet privy. He knows where you'll be going after the game. For you it's a mystery, but he sees the entire scene. He has a bird's-eye view of the parking lot, the surrounding neighborhoods, the roads leading to the highway, leading to a new city, leading to your new home. The route you take after you leave the stadium is all programmed into his GPS. It's been mapped out and carefully thought out. We can't know where we're going when we exit the stadium, but God knows, and we can trust him.

As big as we might think planet Earth is, it is no more than a tiny stadium in the grand scale of creation. Whether we believe in the idea of reincarnation or not, we can accept that beyond this life is another life, and beyond this world is another world, and God has prepared everything perfectly for our arrival. He sees us in these bodies, but he also sees us in our new bodies, in our next lives, and throughout eternity. And what might heaven look like when at last we leave these bodies? Certainly we can expect to connect again with loved ones. We can hope to pick up where we left off, but immersed in love and free from previous roles and expectations. We will not be burdened by troublesome life experiences from our past, as they will be gone, never to hurt us again. If there is something to be learned from a previous life, we will have learned it, or it will be reframed and revisited from a higher, more enlightened perspective. In heaven, all that is left behind will be for our highest good, and all painful things not worth remembering will be forgotten. Forgetting will be freeing.

On Earth the most sublime experiences, the most splendid views, the most beautiful music, the most peaceful feelings, the most precious truths, the most gracious personalities, the happiest occasions—are all foretastes of the heaven which we will one day know. Upon reaching more enlightened realms of existence, we will then experience foretastes of even higher realms of heaven and even grander ways of living. Heaven will unfold continuously just as our lives here on Earth unfold, from year to year and age to age.

We should not think of heaven, though, solely as a future destination when it can also be a present reality. It is not just a resting place prepared for us after death, but a new way of experiencing life now. As Jesus taught, "The kingdom of heaven is within you." But what does that mean, and how can we possibly find heaven inside of ourselves? Heaven breaks into our lives each time we do the will of God, each time we have an unselfish urge to love someone, each time we are kind and generous toward others. Heaven can be found in the feeling of satisfaction that overtakes us when we solve someone's problem, alleviate someone's pain, improve someone's quality of life, offer someone hope, or connect someone to a higher truth. Heaven is our reward for doing God's will, whether knowingly or unknowingly.

Around the world, Christians often pray: "Our Father in heaven, hallowed be your name. Your kingdom come, your will be done, on Earth as it is in heaven." This kingdom is for everyone who seeks it, and it is not meant to be some distant reality. The kingdom to which Jesus referred is the inevitable consequence of connecting with God and loving one another. We should look forward to a more heavenly home after our lives here, but we should also make every attempt to bring heaven to mind, heaven into our homes, and heaven to Earth. We should strive to create a world where all feel welcome, protected, and loved. Then, through loving acts of service and peaceful cooperation, heaven will naturally appear. It will arise from those who are in touch with God's Spirit. It will break through as we quietly go about our day, displaying the fruits of his Spirit—love, joy, peace, patience, kindness, goodness, faithfulness, and self-control.

Slowly God draws us to himself until we take on his character more and more. Gently he guides us, kindly he corrects us, always he forgives us and upholds us. He sees us as already perfect, for time will make it so. Do you think humanity is on a path toward hell? Think again. Perhaps we have only created it within our minds and brought it to life around us. But God will not abandon us to our own creations. In due time he will raise us out of our misery, restore us to our senses, remove our fears, and show us a better way of living. God offers hope for all who have wandered and lost their way. He offers a plan of restoration, reconciliation, rehabilitation, and redemption. If it were not so, we could not call him our Heavenly Parent. For even human parents will show forgiveness and mercy to their children, so how much more will our Heavenly Parent show compassion to all who have lost their way?

If we go back to our stadium, where we are all gathered to observe and play the game of life, pretend that within the stadium, halftime is called, and everyone is allowed to break for an hour of worship. Now imagine that all around the arena, in every corridor and suite and throughout all levels of seating, people get up and regroup with those of similar religious backgrounds and like-minded beliefs. Ushers appear to escort everyone to their desired place within the stadium as sound-proof curtains descend, decorators rush in, color schemes change, chairs are rearranged, alters go up, lights go down, and spaces all around the stadium are magically transformed.

In one area are Catholics having mass, followed at arm's length by Episcopalians, Lutherans, Methodists, Baptists, Presbyterians, Unitarian Universalists, Christian Scientists, Jehovah's Witnesses, Mormons, Pentecostals, and Evangelicals—all worshiping, praying, and singing. Quakers sit in quiet repose. On one end of the field are Shiite Muslims and on the other end Sunni Muslims, all with their prayer rugs facing Mecca. In between are Sufis and Baha'is. In another area Jews are gathered for worship. In another Hindus, side by side with Sikhs, Buddhists, and all manner of faith groups. Agnostics and atheists engage in meditation and open discussions.

In every corner of the stadium, people peacefully congregate for an hour of worship, conversation, and contemplation. Within each group there is something familiar that binds these believers together. The rituals, prayers, music, décor, spoken words and silence all offer a sense of comfort and peace. And this is exactly how it is around the world today. We worship according to our beliefs, traditions, and upbringings, and there are few occasions to mingle with those beyond our curtains. Our separate ways of gathering and worshiping offer us safe, familiar spaces where we can express our inner selves and not feel judged or ridiculed.

But now imagine if there were no curtains to separate us, no rituals to divide us, and no words to hinder a harmonious assembly. We would acknowledge those around us as equals, despite differences in beliefs and outer appearances. Within our hearts we would all simply love God and love one another. Extremism, fanaticism, intolerance, and fear would be absent. Cooperation and unity would prevail. We would be respectful, gracious, and openminded. One group would not dominate or impose their beliefs on the whole. We would listen, learn, and be loving toward all.

The need to defend ourselves and prove ourselves will have passed. There will be no wars, acts of aggression, or belligerent pronouncements. The burden to transform the world into a place of goodwill and peace will have ended. We will be an informed and enlightened society, where we feel safe and accepted among family, friends, and strangers alike. We will have learned how to care for one another and how to care for our world. We will have a truly representative government, and on that day, we will all live with one foot in heaven and one foot on beautiful planet Earth.

Though this day may be thousands of years away, the long journey of transforming Earth into a more heavenly home has already begun. As each generation does its part, and as each individual is able to bear more spiritual fruit, the landscape of our world will change. Today we see a great deal of strife and subdividing of people into various races, nationalities, religions, and political parties. Eventually, though, instead of division and deep-rooted animosities, we will find oneness with God and a unified humanity.

Heaven is our final frontier. God arranged the whole universe so that it evolves toward perfection. With each passing year, with each passing age, heaven unfolds more and more. Now we see it in part, but in time we will see it fully. Like a secret garden, it hides behind an overgrown wall. Most often it is out of view, but on occasion we can discover its beauty. After much searching, we can find the key to the hidden door, pull back the ivy, and enter in.

And, oh, how lovely the garden! How beautiful the landscape! We see flowers and plants of every imaginable kind. It is all so fragrant and enchanting. Yellow daffodils, red azaleas, magenta bougainvillea, purple wisteria, pink dogwoods, weeping willows, poplars, pines, magnolias, and so much more fill the landscape. Cherry blossoms drift through the air. You see a crystal-clear stream, filled with colorful fish and gemstone pebbles. You hear birds singing and the water gently flowing. Sunlight filters through the trees, and there is a perfect blend of sun and shade all around. The air is warm and welcoming, and the lawn so lush and inviting. A host of animals gather round to welcome you. And look, a table has been prepared for you along with a refreshment, so you sit awhile and quietly drink in heaven.

Within each hour are opportunities to experience heaven. Briefly it pops up to color our day. In glimpses it comes our way. It finds us, and we cannot help but be moved. No matter its form or fragrance, we know when it has arrived, for it blesses us and reminds us there is something beautiful within and beyond this world—something softer, gentler, grander, sweeter. For a moment, we escape the difficulties and drudgeries of life to experience the Divine. For a moment, we see the dark clouds part and the light appear to absolve us all.

If we pay attention, we can see heaven arising from within ourselves and within others. We can see it woven into nature and into caring communities. We can see it resting on the faces of the young, elderly, worn out, and weary. We can witness it in small acts of kindness. We can sense it in an awareness of truth and in occasions of pure joy. We can hear it in a mother's voice, a baby's cry, or a widow's sigh. Out of nowhere it can appear like a refreshing rain to remind us we are loved, to summon us to love again, to propel us to serve, and to fill us with peace. Heaven can shine through anywhere, at any hour, if we have the eyes to see it. It can draw us instantly out of the darkness, so let us be careful not to miss it. Let us be on the lookout for something wise and wonderful, something bold and beautiful, something good and gentle, which flows continuously throughout our universe.

God foresaw everything needed for our existence even billions of years ago, before the foundation of the world. In his infinite wisdom, in his ability to see above and beyond time, he knew exactly what would be needed for all living things to survive and thrive. He provided it all and wove it into the evolutionary process. If it were not so, we would not be here.

If God did not love us, or stood at a distance, we would have no reason to hope. But we do hold on to hope, even in the most dire circumstances, even when we cannot see the light, even when our burdens seem too much to bear, because his Spirit lives within us. The Source of all hope resides within our very being. The Designer of all that is good and beautiful dwells within us. We can hold fast to hope because the one who bore the whole universe has placed a fragment of himself within us—to sustain us, comfort us, and fill us with purpose.

If part of our purpose is to help create heaven on Earth, how can we go about doing this, and what might it look like? It looks like loving the whole family of humanity, those here and abroad, and wanting the same privileges for them that you desire for yourself and your own family. It looks like praying for the good fortune and happiness of everyone around the world. It looks like a beloved community. It looks like restoring those who have lost their way and reversing the fate of those who are impoverished, imprisoned, homeless, and helpless. It looks like offering relief to families fleeing war zones and flood zones. It looks like basic human rights and services for all. It looks like clean air and water. It looks like children being raised in loving homes.

It is not enough to identify a problem or to be aware of a crisis. It is not enough to sympathize with someone's pain and suffering. At some point we must be prepared to act, to change, and to help bring about more peaceful living for all. In the end, we are either promoting hell or creating patches of heaven, which can then be woven together for the benefit of all. For it is only when we work together that we can eventually cover the world with love, kindness, peace, and joy.

Pray that heaven will break into your life and show you a better way of living. Ask that you be delivered from an uncaring heart, unclean thinking, or a downcast spirit. Ask to be free of indifference and inaction. Ask God to grant you enthusiasm and energy to change the world around you. Ask him to stir up your heart so you can have compassion on those who are struggling. Ask him to help you bring heaven to mind, heaven into your home, and heaven to Earth.

You have incredible power and potential within you, so do not think you can't make a difference. Imagine a brighter, better world, and then go about your day helping to create that world. Remember, you are a child of God, and he will empower you and help you fulfill your purpose. Pray for guidance, pray for courage, and then trust that he will show you the next step forward. Each step along God's path for your life will lead you one step closer to heaven. On the path there is no need to fear the future or your fellow travelers. Trust God to lead you, and even if you should stray, know you cannot go far, for he has set a limit to your wandering ways. He will soon call you back, so all you will have lost is a little time. Then you can begin again to walk the path he has prepared for you and to be a willing co-creator with God.

Chapter 10

We all make plans in life to carry us through from day to day and year to year. Some plans may seem small and insignificant, while others may appear large and impossible to achieve. They can range from completing a simple task to obtaining a college degree, owning a home, raising a child, becoming more patient, or changing the world.

Maybe your goal is to feel better about yourself or to improve your overall vitality. If so, you might make plans to take up walking, avoid certain foods, drink more water, get more rest, or imagine yourself happy, healthy, and surrounded by friends. Maybe your goal is to get a job with a particular company. If so, you might try to land an entry-level position or accept an internship, knowing you can work your way up the ladder. Or maybe you're interested in dating someone. If so, you might go to great lengths to get to know the person, make a good impression, develop a friendship, and aim for a lasting relationship. Maybe your desire is to become a parent. If so, you might take better care of yourself, discuss plans with a partner, prepare your home, and imagine life as a mom or dad.

In each case, you are setting your sights on a goal and pursuing it strategically. Pursuing heaven on Earth is no different. We can hardly lay claim to it unless we make it a goal. We can discuss the idea of heaven, we can dream about a better way of living, and we can imagine what it might look like in some distant future, but unless we actively pursue it, we can never bring it to pass. The process of transforming our world into a more heavenly home begins within each one of us. It begins by listening to the voice within. It begins with a vision that Earth can be transformed into a happier home, where all can experience greater peace, joy, provision, and freedom. It begins with an understanding that we are all connected. It begins with an acknowledgement that within the body of humanity, when one part suffers, we all suffer.

When we reject all that heaven is not and spend time reflecting on things that are lovely, beautiful, and true, we are actively pursuing heaven. When we make plans, pass laws, and strive to overcome the ills of society, we are inviting heaven to Earth. When we turn away from harsh, aggressive, overly competitive, degrading influences, we are choosing heaven. When we promote healthy, wholesome, joyous living, we are establishing heaven on Earth. When we bless those around us with our thoughts, words, and deeds, we are fulfilling the will of God.

Sometimes, though, we can become so engulfed in our immediate culture that we lose our awareness of and sensitivity to all that God desires for us. When we are exposed to wrong thinking, it's easy for God's voice to be snuffed out. When we are caught up in surroundings that are depressing and demeaning, it's easy to stop hoping, dreaming, smiling, and singing. It's easy to begin internalizing the low expectations placed on us, rather than turning to God for insight and inspiration. In time, no matter what form the darkness takes around us, we start to consider it normal, and we grow accustomed to fearful, joyless living. We accept it as part of God's plan, and day by day we grow weary and weak, slowly losing our way.

Therefore, everyone has a role to play in improving our culture and transforming the world. Whether it's how we conduct ourselves in private or public, how we treat each other, or how we care for animals and the earth, we are all either bringing heaven closer or keeping it at a distance. The politicians we endorse, the professions we choose, the promises we keep, the habits we form, the thoughts we think, the comments we post, the products we use, the food we eat, or any other choices we make—they collectively leave us either starving for heaven or enjoying the fullness thereof.

Heaven on Earth is a way of thinking, a way of acting, and a way of living. It's staying connected to God's Spirit so you can be a better, kinder version of yourself. It's desiring a basic level of dignity for everyone. It's making sure our children are loved, nurtured, and educated in kindness. It's having compassion for all living things. It's giving a voice to the voiceless. It's working to solve problems collectively. It's engaging with others to relieve suffering and end wrongdoing. It's accepting a global unity that transcends nationalism. It's doing what is right, regardless of what is popular or profitable. It's becoming a lighthouse and shining your light on the dark places around you. It's emptying our homes, schools, businesses, and institutions of all that brings us low, shames us, desensitizes us to violence, and harms society.

Heaven on Earth involves spending time each day putting ourselves in other people's shoes and walking around. Have you ever imagined what it might be like to be someone else? To be your partner who is living with you or your kids who are trying their best to balance school life and home life? Or your neighbor who is of another race, ethnicity, or sexual orientation? Imagine if you were a minority or a person in the majority. What if you were far away from home, separated from family, and trying to get by? What if you were a person sitting alone in a prison cell? What if you could not make ends meet or afford to buy food for your family? What if you could never take your children on vacation? Can you sympathize with the hardships others might be experiencing? Can you put yourself in the shoes of someone of another faith? Can you think of them as equals? Can you imagine being someone who is sick, disabled, addicted, homeless, or powerless? Can you imagine just for a moment what they might be going through?

Our first step to entering heaven is discovering what it means to live with a compassionate heart within a caring community. Our second step is accepting that we all have a role to play. In a democracy every person has a vote, and encrypted within each vote is a fragment of an unknown future. Each vote is like a puzzle piece, and when combined with other votes, they form a picture—a new future reality. If you don't vote, the future is altered and the full image of what might have been will never come to light. And just as you can alter the course of a nation by voting, you can also alter society by following the voice within. If you discern an inner voice calling you to defend the defenseless, feed the hungry, teach our children, heal the sick, beautify your surroundings, flee from poisoning influences, or quietly refuse to move to the back of the bus, then you are doing your part to bring heaven to Earth.

One person can make a difference and help heaven gain a foothold. When even one mind awakens or one heart is stirred, a voice can eventually be heard, movements can arise, and harmful dominions can fall like dominoes. Believe that your voice counts. Believe that your vote matters. Believe that your individual thoughts, prayers, decisions, and actions can all have a positive impact on society. When enough people truly want to be good on a personal level and to see improved living on a societal level, then collectively a tipping point will be reached, and change will come to pass; heaven will naturally appear.

As goodness and kindness pour forth from within us, pools of living water are created, and from these pools many can drink and be healed. Families can be refreshed, people restored, institutions reformed, society uplifted, and the earth renewed. Heaven on Earth must first begin within each one of us, though. It must begin with a decision to spend time with God each day, who can calm our thoughts and help us lay down our heavy loads of worry, judgmentalism, and fear. Just a small sacrifice of time, just a short period of prayer or meditation, and then the peace of God will happily unfold around you.

God is always moving us in the direction of perfection, so we should never give the slightest thought to the concept of eternal damnation. We should never assume we are headed to a stadium called hell, where there are no exit doors. The only versions of hell we will ever need to consider are the ones we create for ourselves. But the human-made hells we have created have plenty of exit doors. Hell is never a permanent place. It is a process, a series of unfortunate events and wrong choices, that leads us spiraling in the wrong direction. But at any point, within any realm of hell, no matter how low we have descended, there is a way out; there is an opportunity to call out to God and ask for help.

The steps that lead us away from heaven, from the shore of truth and peaceful living, are numerous and diverse. Some of these steps may have been our own choosing, but some may have been forced upon us by no fault of our own. Maybe you were born into unfavorable circumstances, had a difficult upbringing, or had a home environment that was neither nurturing nor supportive—that's all a step away from the shore, a step away from God's best for your life. Maybe someone you loved suddenly passed away and you felt lost and alone—that's a step out into the water. Maybe you had trouble in school and dropped out—now you're up to your knees. Maybe you couldn't get a job, had too much debt, or became desperate—you're in even deeper. Maybe you got caught up in a lifestyle of drugs and alcohol—you're deeper still. Maybe you had a failed relationship, a breakup, or a divorce, that left you bereft—that's another step away from the shore. Maybe you were mistreated or taken advantage of—you're up to your chest in water. Maybe you lost all sense of reality, all sense of right and wrong—now you're up to your nose. Maybe the shoreline is a distant memory and you've given up all hope of a better life—suddenly you're underwater and you don't know how to swim.

That's hell. It cuts lives short and keeps us trapped in situations or states of mind that prevent us from experiencing the fullness of God's love. But we were not made for hell; we were made for heaven, and at any moment, we can call out to God. We can ask him to rescue us in our moments of desperation and to pull us up from the depths of despair.

God understands all of the trials and temptations that make up our world. He knows how easily we can slip up and give up. He knows how often we can make bad decisions, so for this reason he asks that we make only one decision—the highest decision of all, which in turn will simplify all other decisions. He asks that we decide to let him into our lives. He asks that we choose harmony with him over struggle with the world.

When you turn to God whole-heartedly, rich rewards will always follow. You will learn you never walk alone. You will find your dire circumstances transformed into something brighter and more beautiful. You will see yourself and all those you look upon as holy. You will see all confusion and sorrow swept away until only joy and peace remain.

The process of falling away from God is often long and painful. We don't always know when we are closing the door on God or moving in the wrong direction, but if we pause and pay attention, we can easily read the signs. It may start with a lack of peace, a feeling of sadness, a low-grade depression, or a lingering guilt. It may begin with an unloving thought, a deep resentment, or a hardening of your heart. It may even begin innocently by trying to live up to someone's expectations, trying to fit in with friends, trying to force something to happen, or trying to be perfect with no room for error.

An extreme example of someone who has wandered far from God and silenced the voice within would be a mass murderer. If we could follow such a person back in time, we would see their gradual departure from God's best plan for their lives.

Murderers do not suddenly wake up and for no apparent reason begin killing people. Before the first shot is ever fired, there is often a long series of painful disappointments, quiet sufferings, harmful influences, poor decisions, false conclusions, and twisted thoughts, which eventually lead to acts of terror and violence. But every step of the way there is an opportunity to cry out, however weakly, to a God who can rescue us from complete insanity, depravity and the violent activity that leads to hell on Earth.

As people cry out, we have a responsibility to come to their aid. We cannot distance ourselves from their problems and expect God alone to perform miracles. In partnership with God, we must be the answer to other people's prayers. We must be sympathetic to the suffering around us, the temptations people face, the struggles they daily endure, and we must be willing to act and offer solutions. We must make every effort to provide loving, supportive, nurturing environments long before thoughts of desperation and violence can cross people's minds.

On a societal level, when we elect leaders who wield power and pursue plans without moral considerations, we are opening a door for hell to enter. When we plunder the earth's resources and mistreat wildlife, we are wading in rough waters. When we grow wealthy at the expense of others, we are headed deeper out to sea. When we see inequalities and great gaps in income, education, housing, and health care, the waves have begun to wash over us. When we see mass incarcerations and few opportunities for citizens to improve their lives, we have been carried far out to sea. When we see many slipping into despair, corruption, and crime, we are a long way off from the shore of peaceful living. And one step closer to hell.

As horrible as hell can be, though, it is never permanent. At any given point in time, no matter how dire the situation, you can turn to God and ask for help. If you are sincere and reach out to him, he can turn your life around. And if enough sincere souls reach out to him, he can turn a city around, a country around, even a world around. He can snatch us from beneath the sea and place us on a shore of peaceful living. He can change leaders, policies, laws, and outcomes. He can open our eyes, lead us to higher ground, teach us a better way, and deliver us from hell. No matter how far from the shore we may stray, he can return us to a place of peace. It's never too late to call on God.

Have you ever asked yourself, when you look up at the night sky, or when you hear of the vastness of our universe, if we are really alone? Or are we possibly in the company of millions, billions, or trillions of planets inhabited by intelligent beings? And if we are just one among an innumerable multitude, how do we compare? Are we considered more enlightened, or are we far down on the scale of understanding? Are we closer to hell in the way we care for each other and our planet, or are we closer to heaven?

Surely we know from personal observations, daily living, and news reports that we are still a long way off from perfection. Yet how are we in relation to other worlds? Maybe if contact is eventually made, we will pat ourselves on the back and be proud of our progress, or maybe we will be alarmed by how little we have advanced relative to other worlds. Maybe we will find we are in familiar company, that we are evolving along similar paths and have much in common with our neighbors within the galaxy. Or maybe we will be so awed by an advanced civilization that we will suddenly decide to put aside our differences and work together for the benefit of all. But no matter how we get there, one day we will all know the importance of loving one another, preserving the beauty of our world, caring for all living things, respecting biodiversity, sharing our resources, and working together as one people, one planet, and ultimately, one universe.

Each one of us has an important part to play in the establishment of heaven on Earth, so don't shy away from your responsibility. Begin today to shine brightly, wherever you are. Begin today to make a difference within your personal sphere of influence, however great or small. Begin to stake out a patch of earth that you can transform into a fragrant garden. Maybe your garden will be a private place for only you and your family to visit, or maybe it will grow to be a public space where many will come to find rest and renewal. Whatever you do, do it well, and do it with a happy heart. Do it knowing God has given you this work and only you can do it.

One day, maybe soon or maybe in a distant future, you will be able to look back on planet Earth from the other side, from another home, and you will remember with fondness your time spent here. All your sorrows will be forgotten and all your lessons learned. You will think of Earth and remember the sights and sounds, the places and faces, the family and friends, the work completed. And you will smile knowing you once lived here, you once experienced so much here, and you once did your part to bring heaven to mind, heaven into your home, and heaven to Earth.

Until we are able to transform Earth into a more heavenly abode, we all have work to do. We are not meant to be on permanent vacation. It's fine to put our feet in the sand while on a trip to the beach, but too often we want to bury our heads there too. We want to escape the hard realities of life rather than face them one by one. When the going gets tough, we want to shrink back from our responsibilities, avoid difficult conversations, and put off tough decisions. We procrastinate, turn up the music, eat too much, work too much, worry too much, or numb ourselves with all manner of substances. When all we need to do is quietly go within.

Do you want a fresh outlook on life? Do you want to lift your head out of the sand and be filled with a profound sense of peace and purpose? Do you want to gain a larger vision for your life? All of this can be had when we take time to turn to God on a daily basis. Before your day becomes filled with activity and anxiety, take a few moments to turn to the Presence within. You may be tempted to take care of many important matters and make many important decisions today, but do not neglect the most important decision of all—whether you will allow God into your life. Give him a moment of your time, and then allow all things to fall into place. Such a small sacrifice for such enormous peace of mind.

God has a perfect plan for each of our lives. He has made us each distinct, yet he calls us to live as one. As instruments of his love, he awakens us to our unique abilities while uniting us to play within a full, well-balanced orchestra. He serves as our conductor and helps us color the world with kindness and sweet-sounding music. He uses all that we give him to uplift, inspire, and energize the world around us.

Are you wondering about your role in the orchestra? Are you struggling to find the right direction for your life? Are you questioning whether you have a calling to uncover? Ask God for guidance. Ask who he would have you become. Ask to know the path to follow, the talents to develop, and the goals to pursue. Ask to know the relationships to form—for a season or a lifetime. Ask to be given the courage and discipline needed to live your best possible life.

Within you is the power to lead a calm, balanced, productive, satisfying life. Within you is a blueprint for better living. God did not intend for us to spend our lives filled with anxiety, uncertainty, and fear. With each passing year, he desires that we grow more stable, steadfast, and secure. He desires that we iron out disbelief so we no longer vacillate between hope and doubt or faith and fear. When we accept that we have a Heavenly Parent who loves us, we will no longer overreact or underreact to the events of our lives. We will take the good with the bad, knowing everything will be okay. We will calmly stay the course God is forever revealing to us.

When we're up, and everything is going our way, it's wonderful to appreciate and enjoy life's victories. There's nothing wrong with experiencing intense moments of joy and excitement. But we shouldn't make the mistake of thinking we can ride extreme highs forever. Every big wave eventually breaks and returns to the level of the sea. Every soaring eagle eventually tires and returns home to its nest. Every honeymoon eventually concludes and a new chapter of life begins. Similarly, if you find yourself at an extreme low point, remind yourself that you will return to the level of the sea. If you were once up and now are down, know that this too shall pass. You will not drown beneath the weight of your problems. You will rise above the waters once again and see the light of day.

Sometimes, at the lowest points in life, when we have exhausted ourselves, we can hear the voice of God more clearly.

We can listen without resistance as he whispers words of promise and possibility. We can allow God to breathe life back into us and give us reason to hope. In a flash, he can show us how to put the pieces of our lives back together again. In the blink of an eye he can enlighten us and put us years ahead of where we used to be. In an instant he can change our thinking, our outlook, our attitude, and our plans for the future. Within seconds he can restore our faith and make us happy to be alive. When we least expect it, he can stir us into action. In a heartbeat he can change our fortunes. Out of the blue he can remove an obstacle. And given a little more time, he can transform our world, provide answers to every question, solutions to every problem, and insights into every mystery.

Life on Earth can be full of challenging, exhausting moments. Some days we might be too tired to eat, pray, or love. Other days we might be so overwhelmed by life that we turn our backs on God entirely. But God is never offended by our behavior. He sees all that conspires to crush our spirits, and he is forever working to move us through the pain, to a higher point of understanding and peace. God has the advantage of a long view, an eternal perspective, so though we suffer, he knows the suffering is fleeting and the reward to come immense. Like an athlete in training, we undergo the pain of conditioning in order to be prepared for a greater race and for an eventual victory.

Yet none of that will matter to you when you lose someone close to you, or see a family member suffer or experience a debilitating setback. You will be disheartened when you see acts of violence and injustice. You will be upset when you see cruelty to animals and the destruction of rain forests. You will be disillusioned with God for inventing such a backward planet, for allowing death and permitting pain and suffering. You will despise the wasting away of a loved one, the ongoing addiction of a friend, the loss of a child's innocence, the invention of weapons, the existence of war, the gross economic inequalities, and the persistence of evil. At some point if you're honest, you will hate God, and you will mean it.

But then when you have exhausted yourself and your emotions have died down, you will turn to God and ask why? And if not for his eternal kindness and the supernatural stirring in your soul, you would remain broken. But he would not have you suffer long, and in your greatest moment of pain, you will see that he still comforts you, that he is near. Your eyes of faith will open, and you will see that despite the injustice, the cruelty, the tragedy, the loss, and the finality of it all, there is still more. There is something beyond what you see, hear, and suffer. There is something more beautiful stirring. There is an invisible goodness that does not allow evil to win, trickery to triumph, or darkness to permanently settle. There is a loving Presence who calms, strengthens, and makes all things new.

God will come to you and remind you of all that is lovely and true. He will encourage you, magnify your hope, and give you the strength to stand. He will comfort you when you mourn and guide you when you falter. As you connect with your Heavenly Father and accept that he loves you, everything will begin to change.

As you become more spiritually mature, you will begin to see a shift in your attitudes and desires. You will become less burdened and more hopeful. You will become a problem solver and work to improve the lives of those around you. When you see others anxious and afraid, you will want to heal their minds.

When you see others sick and in pain, you will want to heal their bodies. When you see others hopeless and dejected, you will want to heal their broken spirits. When you see others suffering and facing all manner of hardships, you will want to provide relief, and you will be shown the way.

Maybe in your past, you avoided people you perceived as different. Maybe you distanced yourself from those who were poor, sick, homeless, or dying, not wanting their issues or illnesses to rub off on you. Maybe inner cities, hospitals, prisons, or retirement homes made you uncomfortable. Maybe you looked down on others. Maybe you put up walls around yourself and blocked people off—whole races, genders, age groups, religions, and cultures. Or maybe you looked down on yourself. Maybe you considered yourself inferior in some way—unworthy, unattractive, uneducated, or unqualified. Or maybe you had a perfectly fine self-image and considered yourself blessed and empathetic, but you just didn't want to get involved.

When God calls you, you cannot go back to your old way of living and relating. When he opens your eyes, you cannot help but become a more loving person, a more patient parent, a more concerned citizen, a more awakened individual. As you begin to discern God's voice and trust his inner promptings, he will transform you and call you to higher levels of living and relating. Like water steadily wearing away the hardened features of stone, God will gradually strip you of all that is harsh and uncaring. He will move like a river through the canyons of your mind, forming a kinder, wiser, more lovely you.

Chapter 11

If life is a revolving door of decisions, deadlines, and responsibilities, then you are the doorkeeper. Each day, as the door goes round and round, you can choose to stand by passively and allow everything to flood in and overwhelm you, or you can make conscious decisions about who and what to allow into your life. As the doorkeeper, you can decide which people to let in, which tasks to take on, attitudes to hold, media to view, thoughts to ponder, and priorities to set.

You can guard the door of your life fully awake and fully aware, or you can become a victim of your inner and outer worlds. You can stand at the door calmly and confidently overseeing the flow of events, information, and people as they pass by, or you can go into meltdown mode, and tell yourself it's too much, too difficult, too overwhelming. Avoiding life's many decisions and circumstances, though, is not a strategy for successful living. There may be times when you need to step back, but eventually you must face life head on. There is no point in convincing yourself otherwise because time will not slow down, decisions will not go away, news cycles will not disappear, responsibilities will not stop mounting, and life will not come to a standstill.

And why would you want it to? We're only here for a little while, so we should take full advantage of our opportunities to transform ourselves within and to transform the world without. God made you for such a time as this, so ask yourself each day how you can use your time, talents, energy, personality, and resources to make a positive difference. Ask how you can best serve your family, friends, and community. If you're feeling discouraged or unsure of what you should be doing, know that God will soon enlighten you. Choose to spend time with him each day until you sense his calming presence. Don't give up, and soon you will see your mood lifted, your prayers answered, your confidence restored, and your path made clear.

Certainly each day can have its share of demands and difficulties. Whether it's demands within your family, obligations at work, or events in the outer world, something is always pressing in on us. Maybe a child, an elderly parent, or a pet needs your undivided attention. Maybe an upcoming medical test has you worried, school has you stressed out, technology has you frustrated, a deadline has you irritable, finances are keeping you up at night, or a relationship is wearing you down. Whatever the problem, we should try our best to face each day as optimistically as possible, but don't ever think you must face your problems alone, without the comfort, advice, and support of others. God designed us to live in relationship with him and with each other, so begin today to let others in, to trust God and to lean on family, friends, and sometimes even strangers for support.

When too many hardships come our way, it's easy to lose our sense of peace and lose sight of the Power within. As problems mount, we can naturally withdraw, lash out, or question how we will get through the coming days. If, however, we can focus on the one within, who calms the storms of life, we can get through each day with the courage we need. By maintaining a dialogue with God, we can avoid falling into despair, as he will always lead us to positive outlooks and outcomes.

Day by day, with God as your guide, you can begin to feel less discouraged by the difficulties of life. You can recognize that you do not have to stand idly by and allow things to happen to you. You can accept that you are not a victim of the day's events. You can learn to guard against all that would shatter a peaceful state of mind. You can avoid being rattled by unexpected news, offended by strong personalities, or confused by difficult choices confronting you. You can live more intentionally, calmly deciding which relationships to nurture, which problems to address, and which goals to pursue. You can soar above depression, doubt, and disappointment and become more consistent in character. You can place your faith more and more in the one who is above the difficulties of life.

When we try to resolve life's issues in our own strength and in our own way, we can easily lose our inner joy. We might start out feeling on top of the world, strong enough to handle anything, but then problems mount, pressures intensify, and people make demands on us, until eventually we're worn down by the weight of the world. We can wake up feeling hopeful and energetic but then go to bed feeling drained and defeated. Life is just too complex and filled with too many uncertainties to get through our days without God.

If you find yourself hitting up against a brick wall or suddenly being brought to your knees, it may be because you've been flying solo for too long, excluding God from your life and making plans without him. Don't let a major crisis be what brings you back to God. Stay close to him throughout your day, and spend time developing your relationship, so when the winds of change eventually blow, you will gently bend and not break. It's inevitable that times of testing, sadness, and sorrow will come, but if you know God is by your side, you'll get through the tough times easier, rebound quicker, and move forward stronger than before.

Even if you were born with a sunny personality and are known for your kindness and positive outlook, if you are consistently surrounded by negative people, you can eventually sink to their level. That is why it is important to guard your thoughts and to choose your friends and relations wisely. Sometimes it may mean breaking away from others, either temporarily or permanently, to restore your sense of joy and peace. You have a right to be happy, and you have a God who wants you to be free of guilt, shame, sorrow, and pain.

Becoming free, however, is a process. Unless we are being threatened or injured, it doesn't always mean we should walk out the door when we're upset, overthrow the government when we're angry, or file for a divorce when we want relief. Sometimes we must escape unhappy circumstances by running to God, and trusting that he will help us find a way forward. By turning to God, we can take the burden off of others to make us happy. We can take the burden off of ourselves to be perfect. We can relax, go within, hand our problems over to God, stop overthinking and overanalyzing the details of our lives, and return to a state of perfect peace.

God can give you a peace that passes all understanding, a surety of purpose, and an inner strength that will help you get through each day. He can help you make peace with life despite the challenges you will inevitably face. Life is not meant to be one long holiday, though, because God wants us to have a variety of experiences that will stretch our faith, deepen our character, broaden our horizons, and improve our world. He wants us actively engaged in life—loving, learning, forgiving, serving, building community, and beautifying our world. And this will sometimes involve getting off the easy path of life to exert ourselves. It will require energy, effort, and persistence before our goals can be accomplished, our dreams fulfilled, and heaven realized.

There may be occasions in life when you need to rest and withdraw from your regular routine. You may need to get away from a hectic lifestyle or retreat into nature for a time of calm and quiet. Maybe you need to escape stressful city living, recover from a setback, free your mind, discover God's will for your life, or go through a grieving process following the loss of a loved one. If that's the case, by all means, get away, take a vacation, attend to your own needs, and rest for a season. Don't feel guilty about that, but don't be afraid to reconnect with the world once again when you have recovered.

Life is a great gift, and we should not use our days on Earth to hide away, mourn endlessly, or neglect the work we are called to do. As you rise to meet your responsibilities, God will rise to meet you because he needs your kindness, your energy, your ideas, your talents, your intellect, your voice, your humor, your smile. He needs your loyalty and love. You're of great value to him, your family, your friends, your community, and the world. No matter the highs and lows of life, continue shining and being uniquely you.

We have an unseen world of heavenly helpers cheering us on and ensuring that all things are working together for our highest good. So don't ever think you can't get through the day. Don't ever become so anxious or depressed that you forget all that is good and beautiful about our world. Look around and be thankful. Ask God to help you count your many blessings. Allow him to meet you where you are and to help bring out the best in your personality—all that you will allow.

Prayer, meditation, and contemplation are good and necessary, but you don't need to devote years of your life to finding inner peace. God can meet you anytime, anyplace. You don't need to say long-drawn-out prayers, lead a reclusive life, go on extended fasts, or get a degree in theology to hear from God. You just need a sincere heart and the faith of a child. You just need to talk to God in plain language.

Today we live in a world that is faster, more connected, more complex, and potentially more destructive than ever before. Yet here we are, still going strong. Why? Because we have a keen ability to plunge ahead and prevail in the face of danger and rapid change. As a species we have learned how to adapt, adjust, and transition. We're actually pretty amazing. Evolution did not stop with the dinosaurs, though, or when we learned to walk upright; it continues to push us onward, demanding that we swim and not sink.

In order to continue advancing successfully, we must learn to get along well with others both locally and internationally.

Today we are too interconnected to pursue plans with no thought as to how our values and behavior will affect others. Everything—from the food we eat, to the resources we use, to the money we spend, to the political candidates we support, to the weapons we build, to the media we watch, to the education we offer our children—can have far-reaching consequences. Today our future rests on our ability to be compassionate and mindful of every living thing. It rests on our ability to live as members of one global family.

In previous generations, life was slower and far less connected. Less than 150 years ago, there were no planes, cars, phones, radios, televisions, computers, apps, or internet. You didn't travel far, you didn't travel fast, and you didn't communicate instantly with people around the world. People stayed close to home, and neighbor meant the person who lived nearby—next door, down the road, or within your town. Now neighbor has taken on a whole new meaning. Today people can communicate with someone a continent away as easily as someone a couple of doors away. We are plugged in, making calls, listening to music, checking social media, watching the news, conducting business, playing games, tracking vital signs, riding high-speed trains, and flying through the air. It's hard to imagine what life will be like a few centuries from now.

Change can be exciting, but it can also be scary and unsettling. The thought of change can energize us or cripple us. It all depends upon how we see our place in the universe. If you think life is random, that there is no rhyme or reason to anything, that there is no divine plan, then life can quickly become overwhelming. If, however, you accept that there is a God who loves you, who has a plan for your life, it will start to make sense.

If you accept that God designed you from the beginning to live in a changing world while teaching you to hold fast to a set of changeless values, then you will get through life more easily. If you value faith, friends, and family, then you will find joy and peace sooner than later. If you trust that all things are working together for your highest good and answers to your problems are forthcoming, then you will feel less anxious. If you know you are guided, even when you can't see the next step along the path, then you will be emboldened to move forward. If you believe you will be brought through the storms of life stronger and wiser than before, then you will be just fine.

We live in an imperfect world as imperfect creatures, overseen by One who is perfect. Little by little we are brought closer to his goodness, kindness, and perfection, but the process can be painful. Sometimes we avoid change by running away or returning to old habits, old behaviors, and old stomping grounds. But God wants to move us forward, and he won't allow us to remain stuck in the past for long. Sometimes, if the change is more than we can bear, we go about damaging relationships, wrecking our health, behaving irrationally, and acting out of fear rather than love. When fear is our motivation for anything, we are resisting God's best plan for our lives. So the next time you are confronted with change or news you did not expect, try pushing your fear aside, activating your faith, and remembering the goodness of God.

If we turn to God throughout the day, he will give us a sense of calm in the midst of uncertainty, insight in the midst of confusion, and guidance when we don't know what to do. Take time to listen, to seek his advice, and discern where God is leading you. Choose to make peace with your situation, to soften your heart, to set boundaries if needed, and to act boldly if action is required.

God is actively working within us to shift our attention from the temporal to the timeless. He wants to show us that no matter the challenges we face, regardless of our doubts, despite the fear and setbacks, he is near. There is a world we cannot see with our human eyes, and in that world are all manner of activity and all manner of helpers who aid us even now. Just because we can't see them doesn't mean they don't exist. The human eye has its limits. Our field of vision is infinitesimal compared to the vastness of our universe, and we must learn to trust that God is at work in our lives. Nothing is impossible for him. No situation is hopeless. Even when we draw dire conclusions and grow discouraged, God can intervene to push the clouds away, brighten our day, and remind us to be of good cheer.

The goal of time, the reason God created it, is to provide a means for the gradual growth, transition, and perfection of all things. As humans, we pass from our initial phase as mortal, evolutionary beings to our final phase as divine, spiritual beings within a universe of time and space. Time marks our long journey of progress from Earth to the highest heaven, where at last we achieve timelessness. Our passage through time allows for every stage of living and learning until our personalities are so perfected, our discoveries so amazing, and our love so vast that our minds become the mind of Christ and our spirits become one with God.

We cannot know the exact number of years we will remain on Earth, but because of the existence of time and evolution, we can assume God takes great pleasure in the gradual transformation of all things. He is not rushing to see us fully evolved and fully perfected. Rather, he seems to prefer a gradual, deliberate approach to life. He is doing a work within us that will stand the test of time and sustain us throughout eternity.

God is admiring of everything and in no hurry. He knows the beginning from the end and is surprised by nothing. He is untroubled by delays, shortcomings, and imperfections. He helps the weak become strong. He helps the lowly become lovely. He helps the uncaring become kind. He helps the broken become whole. He is patient and merciful toward every being in his universe. He baffles lesser minds with his ways, but he is devoid of conceit. He does not boast; he is not proud. He is generous and gives endlessly of himself. He respects and protects his creations throughout eternity.

Because life on Earth is progressive, meaning we have developed over millions of years into *Homo sapiens* and then within one lifetime we develop in stages from birth to death, shouldn't we assume that life after death is also progressive? Why should the death of our bodies suddenly land us on the farthest shores of Paradise when we have yet to visit so many islands in between? Certainly it may feel like Paradise after the short, hard lives we have lived here on Earth, but what if our passage from here is just a passage out of one of the hardest and harshest realms of the universe? A graduation to bigger and better things to come? What if we continue to higher and higher realms of enlightenment as we traverse the universal seas? What if the entire universe is designed to delight, educate, and liberate us? What if it is designed to make us more and more Godlike? What if we truly are students and sailors for an eternity?

How exciting to imagine that as we pass through the heavens, we will no longer have to suffer through the extremes found here on Earth. Perhaps now we are in one of the densest and most difficult realms of the universe. After all, we still face disease, disasters, and death. We still see extreme poverty and hunger. We still resort to war and violence. We still fight amongst ourselves. We still destroy nature and show cruelty to animals. We still have a long way to go in distributing resources more equitably and showing kindness to all.

As hard as it may be to admit to ourselves, we are still primitive and barbaric in many ways. It may take thousands of years to solve our problems, blend our communities, shed our fears, abolish our weapons, become more compassionate, and create a true sense of global cooperation. The gap between where we are now and where we want to be may seem great, but time is our friend, and God uses it to reveal his divine plan for all.

The universe is anything but boring. It is a living, breathing, breathtaking creation of which you are both a part and an active participant. So enjoy your life. Enjoy your friends and family. Enjoy each and every day. Know that the bad times and the sad times are but fleeting experiences. In time God will lead us out of all sorrow into joy, out of misery into bliss, out of ignorance into understanding, out of anger into forgiveness, out of selfishness into service, and out of our present trials into peace.

Even now, in the midst of whatever trials or tribulations you may be experiencing, there is a place you can visit and become refreshed. There is a place beyond your present space that offers you relief. It is the borderland, the land between self and spirit. The land between the temporal and the timeless. The land between your present reality and your future home. At this border you can experience the Divine, and if you linger long enough, you can be born anew.

At the border you can encounter true freedom. You can see love in every direction and come to know that God is wholly accepting and does not stand in judgment of you. Here you can taste his marvelous, bountiful, unconditional love. And if you have suffered and been stripped of all joy and hope, these will be returned to you at the border.

If you look back, you will see a land filled with obligations and hardships. But if you look forward, you will feel the warmth of a better place to come. Behind you is a world marked by time, and before you is a realm beyond time. You will want to advance, but while in the body you must only refresh yourself and return because there is still much work to be done. Your life in the body is a gift, and you are part of God's plan, so while the borderland is beautiful, you must eventually return. But you will not be left empty-handed. While at the border, you will be given a peace that passes all understanding, a vision of the person you are meant to be, and insight into the work God is calling you to do during your brief stay on Earth.

So come to the borderland and refresh yourself. Approach the mystery and look out on all that is friendly and true. But do not stay and forget the world you left behind. Rather, return home a better person, a renewed person, a person with a fresh awareness of God and your unity with all. Come home with a mission to do more and to be more.

Throughout the ages there have been many spiritual seekers, mystics, and monks who have approached the Divine in various ways. But you don't have to go to extremes to venture to the borderland. You don't have to suffer a near-death experience, engage in psychedelics, or go on a religious pilgrimage to uncover the truth. God will gladly reveal it to you if only you will ask. His love is freely available within, just waiting to be discovered.

Within you is the borderland where God can meet you and transform you. Within you is the place where he can point you toward a more meaningful life. Within you is the place where he can show you the interconnectedness of all things, give you a new worldview, and have you emerge a lover of self, humanity, and all of creation. Within you is where you can begin to radiate peace and poise, and where you can come close to conquering all fear.

Spending time with God will help you know the loving, invisible protection provided you. You will naturally begin to walk in peace, knowing no weapon formed against you can prosper. You will see there are worse things in life than death of the body; there is the death of truth, the destruction of faith, the loss of all hope, the end of peace, and the absence of loving-kindness. And you will resolve to defend these eternal values with the spirit, strength, and personality provided you.

Earth is our training ground in the plan of upward progression toward Paradise and service in the universe. On Earth we are evolutionary creatures, biological beings who have evolved over time. Our ancestors began life in the salty waters. Yet hundreds of millions of years later, we share an intelligence that puts us a little lower than the angels. God designed us for good from the beginning. He designed us to gradually make the transition from purely materialistic and earthly minded to spiritually minded. He designed us to become God-conscious, creative, and builders of great civilizations. He designed us to solve problems, overcome obstacles, pursue peace, extend kindness, and improve our lives.

Paradise is the nucleus of our universe. The word nucleus means kernel or seed. In biology, the nucleus is the brain or control center of a cell. It coordinates the cell's activity and contains its genetic material or DNA. In physics, the nucleus is the center of an atom, which is a million times smaller than a cell. But whether talking about an atom, a cell, a piece of fruit, or our universe, the nucleus is always the heart of the matter. It is the basis for all substance, growth, reproduction, and life. God's residence in Paradise is the nucleus of all existence, but he is at home everywhere. His Spirit, kindness, control, and creative reach extend throughout the entire universe, so never assume God is isolated from you and your problems. Never think for a moment that he is living somewhere beyond the clouds. He is here, near and dear. He is within you.

God's loving presence is forever with us. Even though he is the creator and maintainer of all reality, he is completely accessible. Even though he is the upholder and controller of the entire universe, he listens to our every word. Even though he is infinite and eternal, has no beginning or ending, he cares for us. God has always been and will always be, and he grants us free will to live forever. Even when our bodies give out, we still live on. We still continue our ascent until at last we reach the highest heaven, where there will be unspeakable love, eternal security, endless beauty, perfected personalities, and undisturbed peace. And even if we reject God or end our lives through confusion of mind or lamentable circumstances, he is merciful and will come to us, clear our minds, and have us choose again. For God loves us all and wishes to bring us home, together at last.

Decide today to come home. Decide to join God right where you are. Home is not where your country, state, town, or dwelling place is. Home is where God is. Home is where love is. You can be anywhere in the universe and find God, but he has placed you here, just where you are, for a reason and a season. Your journey can begin where you find yourself today. Your relationship with the Creator of our whole, wide universe can start now. Use the time God has given you to find peace within, to live in harmony with humanity, and to do your part to bring heaven to Earth. You don't know when you will draw your last breath, so decide to use your time here wisely.

You have many choices throughout your day—what to eat, what to wear, what to watch, what to read, what to do, what to think—but your greatest choice is what to do about God. Will you doubt his existence? Will you ignore his presence? Or will you welcome him into your life? Will you begin a dialogue with him? Will you trust him? Will you begin to discover what he wants for you, your fellow travelers, and all life on the planet?

The choice is ours to make. We are not on autopilot. Our destiny is not set in stone. We have the power to change our thoughts, our course of action, our future. Today, no matter how busy you find yourself, no matter how many problems press in on you, no matter the weather or the circumstances of your life, decide to reach out to God. Decide you want to know God's good and perfect will for your life. Decide you want to make a positive difference while here. Decide you want to join humanity in finding peace for the planet and peace with each other. Decide you want to live free of worry, hardship, hatred, and fear. Decide you want this for everyone.

Wherever you are, you are at home with God, and if you could hear him now, he would remind you that all is well, all things are working together for your highest good, and in time all things will be made new, will be made right, and will be made beautiful, because he loves us.

Reflecting Heaven

Charleston, SC
www.PalmettoPublishing.com

Reflecting Heaven
Copyright © 2022 by Valleau Hopkins

Hardcover ISBN: 979-8-8229-0843-7
Paperback ISBN: 979-8-8229-0844-4
eBook ISBN: 979-8-8229-0845-1

Reflecting Heaven

How to Bring Heaven to Mind,
Heaven into your Home and Heaven to Earth

Valleau Hopkins